Hearing the Silence

A Journey Into Inner Sound and Light

Aman Sheel

India, 2025

Hearing the Silence
First Edition, 2025

Printed in India

This book is a work of spiritual guidance. It reflects the author's understanding and experience and is intended for personal growth and meditation support. The author does not assume any liability for individual outcomes.

For inquiries, permissions, or to contact the author:
amansheel@abhiyantra.in

To the feet of my Guru, in whose silence I found my song.

And to every soul walking the inner path, who dares to listen beyond the noise.

Preface

There are words in this book.

But more importantly, there is silence between them.

This book was not planned. It happened—as all true things do—when the inner flame grew too loud to ignore. What you read here is a reflection of my own path: the confusion, the glimpses, the grace, the resistance, and above all, the longing.

This is not a spiritual manual. It is a companion for those who sit quietly in the dark, who listen for a sound not made by any hand, and who sometimes cry without knowing why.

Hearing the Silence is for anyone who has been touched by the inner world, who has felt the pull of something higher, and who knows that the true journey begins not with effort—but with surrender.

I offer this not as an expert, but as a fellow traveler. May Maalik guide each reader deeper into the light within.

Contents

Came as dust, forgotten skies,
Sent down to help, to heal, to rise.
A bhakt once born of flame and grace,
Now wears the veil of time and place.

World was noise, the path unclear,
Till one day the Maalik, near.
Eyes met eyes, and in that gaze,
The soul remembered ancient days.

A flood of lifetimes rushed within,
The work, the vow, the fall, the sin.
But none could blur what burned so true—
The bond no death or birth could undo.

Fell—no pride, no fear, no shame,
Just longing deep, just Maalik's name.
Tears poured forth like sacred rain,
A heart awakened by old pain.

Wept not out of loss or lack,
But joy of finding his way back.
To see his Guru here, so real,
Was more than words could ever feel.

"O Maalik," cried the soul reborn,
"Why did I ever feel forlorn?
You've been breath beneath my breath,
hand that held through life and death."

The Guru smiled, no word was said,
Yet truth was spoken soul to head.
"You came to serve, now rise and be,
A light for those who cannot see."

But still he wept, the bhakt so small,
Before the One who knows it all.
For love like this, so pure, so wide,
No ocean holds, no world can hide.

He cried because he knew at last—
The veil had lifted from the past.
This was the Face he always sought,
This was the Home the soul forgot.

Not mother now, but Maalik true,
Who births the self in light anew.
And every tear a sacred flame,
That sings the Maalik's silent name.

Let others call it weakness, loss—
He knows the path, he bears the cross.
And in his cry, the world will see,
What love for Maalik's meant to be

Anhad Naad

Anhad Naad, also known as Brahma Naad or Surat Shabd Yoga. These practices, despite different names, all aim to help you hear divine inner sounds during meditation. Beginners often get confused about how to listen to these sounds or focus on them correctly. Let's break it down simply to avoid mistakes, as focusing the wrong way can cause physical discomfort.

Clearing Up Confusion

Some people ask that these divine sounds—like flutes, bells, or drums—can't be heard for certain reasons or are different from what's described, and you're not wrong! In deep meditation, you might hear those vivid sounds, but they don't just appear without practice. You won't sit down one day and instantly hear a divine orchestra. Instead, you start with basic inner sounds from lower energy centers, and with practice, you'll hear those beautiful, indescribable divine sounds. Even the basic sounds can lift your focus and prepare your mind for the higher ones.

How to Practice

When you sit for meditation:

1. **Start with a mantra**: Chant to calm your mind and reduce stray thoughts. Stop once your mind feels steady.
2. **Block external noise**: Early on, noises like fans can distract you. Use fingers in your ears, earplugs, or foam ear covers to help focus on inner sounds. With practice, you'll hear these sounds clearly, even in noisy places.
3. **Listen for basic sounds**: These might include:
     - A steady, faint whistle-like sound, continuous without breaks.
     - A sound like crickets chirping in a quiet night.
     - A hum like old telephone poles or a weak radio signal.
     - Chirping like a few birds, then a whole flock.
     - Sounds like flowing water or ocean waves. These vary based on your focus but are common starting points.

How to Focus

You might hear a sound from your left or right ear, sometimes louder on one side. Don't focus on that side—it's not coming from your ears but from the center of your forehead (third eye point). Focusing on one side can strain your eyes or cause physical tension, like a stretched leg or lifted knee, which disrupts your meditation.

Instead, always focus on the sound as if it's coming from your forehead's center. At first, it might seem like no sound is there, but keep your attention there. With practice, you'll feel the sound originates from the center, avoiding strain or discomfort. If the sound fades, return to your mantra to refocus, then try again.

Why It Matters

Centering your focus on the forehead lifts your awareness, making your body feel light and empty. You'll meditate for hours without noticing time. These basic sounds lead you to the divine Anhad Naad. Practice daily, treating the sound like you're searching for its source. Keep your focus in the center, no matter how loud it seems from one side.

This should help anyone stuck on how to focus or which sounds to listen for.

Anhad Naad Explained

Anhad Naad—also called Om, Ongkar, Shabd, or Satnam. Whether you're practicing Anhad Naad Sadhana and feeling stuck or have questions about why your progress seems stalled, let's clear things up in a simple way. We'll cover what Anhad Naad is, why it's called Anahat, the role of mantras, who can hear it, whether you need hours of meditation, how to recognize it, the cricket-like sound mystery, and which sound to focus on.

What Is Anhad Naad, and Why Anahat?

We hear two types of music daily: one from instruments, like a drum that sounds when struck, and another from recordings that stop when powered off. Both rely on something being hit or powered. Anhad Naad, though, is a divine sound humming inside you 24/7 without any external cause. That's why it's called "Anahat," meaning "unstruck." Unlike a drum or speaker, it has no limits and never stops. It's been playing since the universe began, a fact even science's Big Bang theory supports with its idea of a primal sound.

This sound has many names across traditions: Guru Nanak's Satnam or Ek Ongkar, the Vedas' Om or Devvani, Kabir's Shabd, Sufi mystics' Kalam-e-Ilahi, and Jesus' Word. It's the same eternal music, just described differently.

Which Mantra Connects You to Anhad Naad?

Some claim a specific mantra makes you hear Anhad Naad, but that's not true. Mantras calm your mind and guide it to stillness, like a journey to a thought-free state. After chanting (japa), you might reach effortless chanting (ajapa japa) or see divine light. The light and Anhad Naad share the same source, but to hear the sound, you practice Naad Sadhana or Shabd Yoga.

Is Anhad Naad Only for Meditators or Religious People?

This divine sound plays inside everyone, always. Saints say it's a constant hum within us. Even non-meditators sometimes hear it in quiet moments, like when reading or focusing deeply on a task. They might think it's tinnitus, but it's often the result of past-life spiritual practices.

Do You Need Hours of Meditation?

Not at all. Start by listening for a few minutes before bed. You might fall asleep doing it. Daily practice builds a habit you'll love, like a blessing. With time, you'll hear it even in noisy places.

How Do You Recognize Anhad Naad?

You may hear about sounds like flutes, bells, or drums, but those come later. Begin by focusing on the center of your forehead (third eye) for a few minutes daily, ideally before bed or after waking. The sound will draw you inward, and soon, you'll notice life-changing effects.

What's the Cricket-Like Sound?

In Naad Sadhana, people mention a cricket-like sound. It can seem harsh at first, like an alarm, but the real inner sound is soothing. It's compared to crickets because it may resemble a soft hum, like a quiet night. Saints use this example to make it relatable.

Which Sound to Focus On?

At first, the sound might seem to come from your right or left ear, or vary in volume. Don't chase it side to side—that stalls progress. Focus only on the center of your forehead. Soon, the sounds will merge into one, coming from the center. Your meditation will deepen, and you'll sit longer without restlessness. The initial cricket hum may turn into bird chirps, then bells or flutes. Always keep your focus centered, no matter the sound. Chasing it left or right weakens it and stops progress.

Practice daily, focusing on the forehead's center, and you'll connect deeply with Anhad Naad, transforming your meditation and life.

Focusing on the Third Eye

Finding the Third Eye Point

Beginners often wonder where the third eye is—between the eyes or in the middle of the forehead? Some focus on a spot between their eyes, others on the forehead's outer skin, and some roll their eyes upward, thinking that's the key. At first, this might feel okay, but forcing your eyes or forehead creates tension or vibrations. You might hear that tingling or buzzing means your third eye is opening, so you focus harder on it. It feels great initially, but that sensation can turn into pain that lingers all day.

Here's the easy way to focus on the Ajna Chakra. Sit in a comfortable meditation posture. Use earplugs to block outside noise, as total silence is rare these days. Close your eyes gently and don't rush into chanting a mantra or simran (like "Soham"). Take 30 seconds to a minute to let your nervous system settle. Silently pray to your guru, deity, or the divine, asking for guidance and acceptance of your effort to connect with their love. This calms your energy.

In meditation, your body uses three powers: seeing, thinking, and hearing. You don't need to pinpoint a spot between your eyes or on your forehead. This method will guide you to the third eye automatically:

1. **Seeing**: With eyes closed, look into the darkness behind them as if gazing straight ahead, like you would normally. Don't strain or search for anything—just look naturally.

2. **Thinking**: Silently chant a mantra or simran in your mind, like "Soham" or whatever your guru has initiated you with.

3. **Hearing**: As you chant mentally, listen to the mantra in your inner ear. For example, hear "soham" as you repeat it.

Using all three powers—looking, chanting, and listening—keeps your mind fully engaged, leaving no room for wandering. Your eyes will stop darting around, settling naturally. After a few minutes, the mantra's words may fade, and your focus will deepen into the chanting itself. Without effort, your attention will land on the third eye.

Deepening the Practice

With daily practice, your focus will settle on the third eye the moment you sit, without trying. Over time, your eyeballs will gently lift upward naturally. Your awareness will detach from your lower body, which may feel numb from feet to forehead, leaving only the area above your eyes active. This is how you master the Ajna Chakra without strain.

To reach meditation's peak or divine love, don't force your body. In that ultimate state, the body becomes irrelevant, so avoid stressing your nervous system or chasing sensations.

Is It Real or Imagination?

Regular meditation can stir up subconscious thoughts, leading to vivid images or scenes. These might feel spiritual, but if you're aware of any body part—even your eyes—your meditation hasn't transcended the mind yet. Test it by trying to move a finger. If it moves easily, it's likely your mind's illusion. Greet the experience with love, let it go, and return to chanting and listening.

Meditation is a lifelong journey. Practice daily with patience and love. This method will quiet wandering thoughts, guiding you to the third eye and deeper spiritual experiences effortlessly.

Five Key Meditation Experiences

Five important experiences you might encounter during meditation that are actually great signs of progress on your spiritual journey. These moments can feel intense, and both new and experienced practitioners might mistake them for physical issues or worry they're off track. This can stall your progress as you try to make sense of them.

1. Numbness in Legs and Feet

Many think sitting cross-legged stops blood flow, causing tingling or numbness in legs and feet. Here's the truth: blood flow continues, even after hours of meditation. Numbness comes from your energy and awareness shifting as you focus deeply. You might feel this even when lying down with straight legs—feet go numb first, then the whole body. This is a normal, positive sign that you're settling into your meditation posture correctly. It's harmless, so embrace it as your first milestone.

2. Dizziness or Spinning Sensations

You might feel dizzy, like your head is spinning or you're about to fall. When you open your eyes, you're steady, but closing them brings unease. Don't worry! This happens because your body's energy, which normally flows downward, starts moving upward during meditation as you focus on a mantra or Anhad Naad. Your nervous system isn't used to this surge, causing dizziness or nausea. With daily practice, this fades, and you move forward. It's normal, so keep going.

3. Heavy Arms and Shoulders

Your legs may feel numb, but your arms, shoulders, and upper body might feel heavy or stiff, like something is pressing down. You might fear an external force is taking over or that you won't move again. This is a good sign—your body is preparing for longer meditation sessions. Stay focused on the Ajna Chakra (third eye) and keep chanting your mantra or listening to Anhad Naad. This heaviness shows progress, so stay calm and continue.

4. Tingling and Energy Surges

Your body may feel alive with tingling or vibrations, with energy rushing upward from your lower body. You might feel jolts and blissful sensations, but these can break your focus. This tingling might happen outside meditation—while working, at home, or even sleeping. Don't worry if you're doing it right. To reach the next stage, gather your energy toward the Ajna Chakra. These sensations are part of that process. Keep focusing on the third eye, and soon only the area above your eyes will feel active.

5.   Weightless,   Floating Sensation

You may lose all sense of your body, feeling completely numb and light, like you're floating. This is exciting but can be scary—your mind might worry your soul is leaving your body, pulling you back to external thoughts. Don't linger in this excitement or fear. Refocus on your mantra or Anhad Naad with full concentration. Your body is safe, and this stage means you're nearing the next level.

Moving   Forward   with Confidence

These stages—numbness, dizziness, heaviness, tingling, and weightlessness—are normal and show you're progressing. Don't let fear or confusion stop you. If you feel stuck, return to your mantra or Anhad Naad, focusing on the Ajna Chakra. In the final stage, you'll enter a state where body and mind fade, letting you meditate for hours in joy. Every practitioner moves through these stages step by step, each a sign of progress. Practice with patience and love, and you'll advance on your spiritual path without doubt or discomfort.

Mastering Mantra Chanting

You might have heard from saints or others about methods like chanting out loud, syncing with your breath, splitting a mantra into parts for inhaling and exhaling, or chanting silently in your mind. It's easy to wonder which is best. Some folks, even after years, feel no joy or progress and notice discomfort like a stiff neck or sore face.

Why Chanting Feels Mechanical

Repeating a mantra can feel robotic for beginners, with no joy. That's okay! The biggest hurdles in meditation are your restless mind and body. Chanting aims to move you beyond both, connecting you to divine light or *Anhad Naad*. Your mind races like a car, with thoughts—wanted or not—scattering your attention. Sitting with closed eyes calms your senses, but taming your mind takes time. Like a speeding car can't make a sharp U-turn without crashing, your mind needs to slow down gradually. Mantra chanting does just that, helping you focus inward.

Chanting Out Loud: For Beginners

If you're new, start by chanting your mantra out loud. This pulls your focus from the world to a single word or phrase. Saying and hearing the mantra trains your mind to center. But you'll tire quickly, and you shouldn't force it. When your mind feels settled, stop chanting out loud. The mantra will echo silently in your mind—that's when you shift to silent chanting. Forcing loud chanting can strain your neck or jaw, keeping your focus on your body. The goal isn't to hit a chanting quota but to detach from mind and body. Gradually reduce loud chanting time and increase silent chanting to stay calm and turn inward.

Chanting with Breath: A Step Further

This method involves chanting with your breath—either the full mantra on an inhale or exhale, or splitting it, like "so" on inhale and "ham" on exhale for "soham." Some use "Ram Ram". This is a step beyond loud chanting, as it shifts focus from external body parts (mouth, ears) to internal breathing, closer to your mind.
Watch out for:

- **Wandering Thoughts**: A stray thought might pull you away. Jumping back to breath chanting without noticing your breath's rhythm can disrupt it, causing tension or deep breaths.

- **Changing Speed**: If thoughts overwhelm you, you might chant faster or slower, unintentionally altering your breathing pace.

- **Natural Slowing**: As focus deepens, your breathing and heartbeat slow naturally, bringing joy. Forcing long breaths here disrupts your spiritual energy.

Prolonged forcing can lead to discomfort or health issues. When you feel tingling, heaviness, numbness, or slower breathing, your focus is shifting to the third eye (*Dasham Dwar*). The mantra continues silently. Don't pull focus back to your breath—stay at the third eye. The breath method has done its job.

Moving to Silent Chanting

With silent chanting at the third eye, you might feel like you're slipping into deep sleep or that breathing has stopped. Don't worry—your breath slows but never stops. Flow with the mantra. Forcing focus back to breath or loud chanting stalls progress, making it hard to reach the third eye. This can take months or years, with your meditation breaking repeatedly, feeling like two steps forward, ten back. Gradually reduce breath-based chanting as focus strengthens, shifting to silent chanting at the third eye to prepare for *Anhad Naad* or divine light.

The True Goal of Chanting

Chanting isn't the goal—it's the first step. Each method guides you to the third eye, not to keep you chanting forever. True meditation starts when chanting fades, and you transcend body, mind, and illusions. Only your true self, the divine, *Anhad Naad*, and divine light remain. Don't get stuck in loud or breath-based chanting, even after years. They're tools to reach the divine within. Practice with love and faith, moving step by step on your inner journey.

Navigating Inner Sounds in Anhad Naad Sadhana

When you start, you might hear a single sound, like a cricket's chirp, a faint whistle, a quiet hum, or a mysterious echo. Later, multiple sounds may arise together, which can be confusing. Which do you focus on, and which do you let go?

Understanding the Inner Sounds

In *Anhad Naad Sadhana*, you'll first hear basic sounds—a cricket-like chirp, a silent hum, a sharp whistle, or an indescribable echo. Don't think these are unimportant compared to "higher" sounds like bells or flutes. Every sound you hear matches your current meditation stage and is vital. Those grande sounds—like bells, conches, or drums—come in deeper focus, but you need to start with these basic sounds. They gather your awareness to the *Ajna Chakra* (third eye), paving the way for divine sounds later.

Choosing the Right Sound

As your meditation deepens, you might hear multiple sounds at once, leaving you unsure which to follow. Focus on the sound that feels loudest or clearest at the center of your forehead (third eye). At first, even here, sounds may shift—hum, whistle, or chirp. That's okay. Choose the sound that triggers tingling or slight vibrations in your body, like in your legs or back. This sound is pulling your energy upward to the *Ajna Chakra*. Ignore other sounds, even if they hum from your right or left ear. Stay with the one causing physical sensations—it's your guide forward.

Why This Sound Matters

The tingling or vibrations are natural, showing your energy is moving upward—a key part of *Anhad Naad Sadhana*. Don't fear these sensations; they're a positive sign. This sound leads you to deeper stages. If sensations distract you, gently return your focus to the sound at the third eye. With practice, these physical feelings fade as your energy stabilizes. If you hear one sound, listen to it from the forehead's center, even if it seems to come from an ear. Over time, all sounds will feel centered, becoming clear and soothing.

Overcoming Distractions

Early on, these sounds might feel loud or distracting, even keeping you up at night. This happens when your focus isn't steady. With daily practice, as the sounds settle at the third eye, distractions stop, and you'll enjoy listening to them. You'll hear higher sounds—like bells or flutes—later, but for now, the sound you hear is your most important guide. Listen with love and devotion.

Moving Toward Deeper Meditation

Mantra chanting takes you only so far. To reach a state where time and body vanish, *Anhad Naad* and divine light guide you. The sound you hear now is your bridge, deepening focus and extending meditation time effortlessly.

Handling Physical Sensations in Meditation

You might feel changes or discomforts in your body during meditation, how to handle them so they don't derail your practice. Many practitioners focus on reaching meditation's ultimate state but get scared or confused by physical sensations, mistaking them for illness or giving up entirely. Some limit their practice, like cutting meditation to 20 minutes to avoid issues.

Why These Sensations Happen

Your body's energy—call it consciousness or life force—powers daily activities like talking or working, flowing downward. In meditation, as you sit still and focus on the third eye (*Ajna Chakra*) with mantra chanting or *naam simran*, this energy stops flowing outward and reverses upward, from toes to head. This shift, opposite to how energy has moved since birth, causes sensations. Without understanding, you might think they're problems and stop meditating. Let's break these into three categories to understand and resolve them.

Category 1: Head and Face Sensations

Sensations:

- Headaches or heaviness
- Tension at the third eye
- Facial sweating or warmth
- Restlessness or irritation

Why: Early on, forcing focus on the third eye creates tension or headaches. Your head isn't used to this energy surge, causing warmth or restlessness. Persistent discomfort after meditation signals excessive effort.

Solution: Chant your mantra naturally, without straining your eyes or forehead. Don't search the darkness behind your eyes. These sensations are normal as your head adjusts. If discomfort arises, focus on your mantra or *Anhad Naad*, not the sensation. Within days, the tension or heaviness fades. Practice gently and don't worry.

Category 2: Breathing and Heart Sensations

Sensations:

- Tight throat or breathing difficulty

- Slow or "stopped" breathing
- Increased heartbeat
- Heavy hands, neck, or shoulders
- Something passing through the throat upward

Why: As energy gathers to your shoulders, the lower body needs less, slowing breathing and heartbeat. If focus breaks (e.g., from a noise or thought), energy rushes back, causing deep breaths or a racing heart, making you fear health issues. Energy moving through your throat feels tight or stiff.

Solution: Don't force breathing, especially in breath-based meditation, to avoid disrupting its rhythm. If you feel tightness or a fast heartbeat, return focus to the third eye with your mantra or *Anhad Naad*. Your breath slows but never stops. With practice, these sensations normalize. Stay calm and keep going.

Category 3: Body-Wide Sensations

Sensations:

- Tingling or vibrations
- Jolts from feet to head
- Churning in stomach or chest
- Body swaying or internal movement

Why: Energy hitting blockages causes tingling or jolts. Strong focus amplifies energy, leading to jolts that break meditation, with fast breathing and heart rate. Weaker energy causes warmth or movement in legs, waist, or chest.

Solution: Don't focus on jolts or tingling—return to the third eye with your mantra or *Anhad Naad*. These persist until blockages clear with practice. Stopping here keeps you stuck. Call on your guru or divine with love, and focus upward. Sensations will fade, and you'll progress.

Moving Forward with Confidence

Like starting exercise, your body aches at first but adapts. Meditation's upward energy flow is new, causing discomfort, but it adjusts with practice. Don't stall by worrying about sensations—your meditation will stay stuck. Practice with love and faith, focusing on the third eye without forcing. These sensations—headaches, slow breathing, jolts—are normal signs of progress. Soon, energy will flow smoothly, and discomforts will vanish, deepening your meditation toward the divine state.

Understanding Samadhi in Meditation

Samadhi—what it is, how you move from meditation to samadhi, what it feels like, when you might see your guru or the divine, and how far you can go without a guru's initiation. This is the moment every practitioner strives for, where meditation truly blossoms.

What Is Samadhi?

Simply put, samadhi is experiencing death while alive. Life's greatest fear is death, and the unknown beyond it is even scarier. In samadhi, you gain this ultimate knowledge, freeing you from death's fear and life's sorrows, pains, and struggles. It's not just meditation's goal—it's the start of your true spiritual journey. The wisdom of saints—about the soul or divine truth—becomes your lived experience. You discover your practice's fruits in this life, not after death. Samadhi has two stages, and all prior meditation experiences—like sensations or sounds—are mere steps toward this peak, reached through daily effort amid worldly duties.

The First Stage of Samadhi

The first stage feels like deep meditation, where you experience boundless peace without specific sensations, just timeless calm. With daily practice, you enter samadhi's first stage, fully awake within. You might find yourself in another realm, even seeing your body meditating. This can be scary—some fear they've left their body—but your consciousness stays linked. Known as an out-of-body experience, this stage confirms your true essence is your soul, not your body.

Here, you may see your chosen deity, guru, or divine presence. Initiated practitioners see their guru; those without initiation may see their destined guru. This is the furthest you can go without a guru. Beyond this, a guru's guidance is essential. Reaching this stage depends on your practice and mental state, guided by divine light and *Anhad Naad*, with joyful experiences along the way.

The Second Stage: Complete Samadhi

With practice in the first stage, divine grace and your guru's blessings prepare you for complete samadhi. You've been immersed in *Anhad Naad*'s divine sounds and divine light, which feel blissful. Suddenly, these forces pull you strongly, like you're merging with them. Despite deep meditation, fear arises—it feels like dying or falling into a dark abyss. Your body may sweat or shake, urging you to open your eyes to check if you're alive.

This tests your trust in your guru and divine. Only a heart full of selfless love and longing for truth can surrender. Saints emphasize love (*prem*) and longing (*virah*) for this reason—they fuel your courage to leap, like a moth to a flame. With your guru's grace, a divine voice might say, "Come, don't fear, I'm with you." Driven by love, you take the plunge, and the universe welcomes you. Tears flow as your soul, separated for lifetimes, starts its journey home. Words fall short here—it's indescribable.

The Leap Beyond

In stillness deep, where silence sings,
You've walked the path of lesser things—
With practice strong and heart made pure,
Prepared by grace to now endure.

The Anhad Naad—celestial sound,
A light within, so vast, unbound.
Its pull so fierce, it draws you near,
A joy divine, yet touched with fear.

Though bliss surrounds like gentle rain,
A shadow creeps—unspoken pain.
The self dissolves, the known must fall,
As death-like tremors grip it all.

Your hands may sweat, your body shake,
The eyes may flutter, half-awake.
Abyss below, unknown above—
This is the test of truth and love.

Here reason ends, here trust must rise,
Beyond the grasp of earthly ties.
What keeps you now upon this brink?
Not thought—but Love's unyielding link.

The saints have known, the saints have cried,
That prem and virah must abide—
A moth consumed within the flame,
Yet gladly flies, and speaks no blame.

Then—soft, within your silent core,
A voice divine: "Fear not, I'm more.
I am the Light, the Sound, the Way—
I've never left. I'm here. I stay."

And with that word, your soul takes flight,
No longer bound by death or night.
You leap, not falling—but set free,
And find the sky's infinity.

Tears spill not from sorrow's gate,
But joy too vast to hold or state.
The journey home at last begun,
Where soul and Source return as One.

No poet's pen, no seeker's prose
Can speak the place where longing goes.
But trust, and love, and leap you must—
And leave the rest to grace and dust.

If you're not at these stages, practice daily with love. Each step nears the first stage. Challenges are universal for those seeking the divine. If nearing complete samadhi, know these intense moments are shared by all who reach this point. Surrender to divine light and *Anhad Naad* with faith in your guru or divine. Love and longing will guide you.

Without a guru, you can reach the first stage, gaining profound insights. Beyond, a guru is vital for navigating complete samadhi's energies. Practice patiently—once you reach the first stage, no force can stop this life's fulfillment.

Let's explore the benefits of listening to *Anhad Naad*—the divine inner sounds—in meditation. Many practitioners ask why these sounds matter, from the basic ones like a cricket's chirp, a quiet hum, a whistle, or a thunder-like rumble, to the higher sounds of bells, conches, flutes, or drums. Often, the initial sounds are dismissed as ordinary, but they're powerful when approached with love, faith, and devotion.

Why *Anhad Naad* Matters

Just as a meditator needs the right physical posture, the mind's state—free from disruptive thoughts—is even more crucial to reach the peak of spiritual practice. The mind's five enemies (*panch vikara*)—lust (*kaam*), anger (*krodh*), greed (*lobh*), attachment (*moh*), and ego (*ahankaar*)—are the biggest barriers. Even great meditators with spiritual powers can fall if these vices take over, ruining both their worldly and spiritual lives. While everyone knows these traits are harmful and tries to control them with intellect, this only works to a point. When your grip on the mind weakens, these vices sneak back in. *Anhad Naad Sadhana* is a powerful way to master them, cleansing your mind and paving the way for spiritual growth.

Benefits of Listening to *Anhad Naad*

When you meditate on *Anhad Naad*'s divine sounds, they quietly transform you from within. As you start finding joy and bliss in these sounds, you change mentally and emotionally without even realizing it. Here's how:

1. **Calming Lust (*Kaam*)**: The sounds reduce lustful thoughts, calming inappropriate desires for others. You become more peaceful and centered, less swayed by physical urges.

2. **Taming Anger (*Krodh*)**: If you're prone to anger, *Anhad Naad* helps you stay calm. Over time, even triggers that once set you off lose their power, and you respond with serenity.
3. **Reducing Greed (*Lobh*)**: The craving for material wealth or possessions fades. You lose the drive to hoard money or chase worldly gains, finding contentment in what you have.
4. **Easing Attachment (*Moh*)**: Grief from losing loved ones or longing for their presence can linger like a wound. *Anhad Naad* gently lifts you beyond this pain, helping you find peace and acceptance.
5. **Dissolving Ego (*Ahankaar*)**: Ego blinds you to life's true purpose. These sounds encourage introspection, making you quieter and more reflective. You start analyzing your actions, gaining clarity to make wiser decisions.

These changes make you more sensitive to life, improving your relationships and worldly responsibilities. You handle family and work with calm and clarity, bringing peace to both your spiritual and everyday life.

Enhancing Daily Life

Anhad Naad inspires you to stay diligent, reducing laziness. The bliss you feel while listening to these sounds lingers, motivating you to complete tasks efficiently to make time for meditation without interruptions. As you progress, worldly pleasures and pains start feeling like a fleeting show. You grow resilient, unshaken by even the greatest sorrows, focusing on your duties and surrendering outcomes to the divine will.

Path to Samadhi

To reach *samadhi*—the ultimate meditative state—you need complete surrender to the divine, which is impossible while the five vices linger. *Anhad Naad Sadhana* purifies your mind, fostering this surrender. As Kabir says, the path of divine love is so narrow that only one can pass—either your ego or the divine. When you let go of self, merging with divine love through *Anhad Naad*, you attain self-realization and divine visions, possible only in *samadhi*.

With regular practice, *Anhad Naad* cleanses your mind (*chitta shuddhi*), as described in the Vedas. You may find yourself crying during meditation, overwhelmed by divine love or regret for past actions. These tears purify your heart, removing deceit and ego, preparing you for divine connection. The divine speaks only the language of love, and *Anhad Naad*, alongside divine light, is the bridge to that union.

A Unified Path

Don't separate *Anhad Naad* and divine light—they come from the same divine source. Some experience the light first, others hear higher sounds; both lead to the same destination. Reflect on this: every worry or pain in life ties back to one of the five vices. To free yourself, meditate daily on *Anhad Naad*'s sounds with love and faith. Even the basic sounds, like a chirp or hum, work wonders when approached with devotion. Over time, others will notice your transformation—your inner peace and strength will shine through.

The Confusion Around Right Ear vs. Third Eye

When you start *Anhad Naad Sadhana*, you might hear sounds from the left ear, right ear, or both, which is common in the early stages. This can break your focus, as you wonder which sound to follow or if you're doing something wrong. If you fixate on hearing sounds only from the right ear, your meditation may stall, and you might even feel physical discomfort, like leg pain, back pain, or tension on one side of your head or body. Let's unpack why the "right ear" idea exists and why focusing on the *Ajna Chakra* is often the better path for householders.

Religious Context of Listening from the Right Ear

To understand the "right ear" advice, we need to look at ancient texts and saintly teachings, as some practitioners may not trust personal experience alone. There are three ways to find answers: ancient scriptures (Vedas, Puranas, Upanishads), teachings of saints across traditions, or insights from an experienced practitioner. I'll focus on the religious perspective to clear your doubts, but this requires careful attention, as studying these texts yourself could take years.

Common Ground in Scriptures and Teachings

All Vedic texts and saints agree on two key points about *Anhad Naad*:

1. **The Divine Sound**: The Vedas, Upanishads, and Puranas describe *Om* as the universe's highest, truest power. Saints call it *Onkar*, *Anhad Naad*, *Shabd*, or *Naam*, while Sufi mystics refer to it as *Aasmani Awaz* or *Kalam-e-Ilahi*. It's the same divine sound, named differently across traditions.
2. **Beyond Physical Ears**: *Anhad Naad* cannot be heard with physical ears. To perceive it, you must gather your consciousness from the body's nine openings (two eyes, two ears, two nostrils, mouth, and two excretory organs) to the

Ajna Chakra (third eye, *Dasham Dwar*). Only through focused meditation can you hear this divine sound.

The "Right Ear" Reference

The advice to hear *Anhad Naad* from the right ear appears in three texts: *Shiva Purana*, *Shiva Samhita*, and *Hatha Yoga Pradipika*. These texts briefly mention closing both ears with fingers and listening to *Anhad Naad* from the right ear. The source for this practice is traced to the *Nadabindu Upanishad*, one of the 108 Upanishads compiled by Shankaracharya, which distills Vedic meditation knowledge.

In the *Nadabindu Upanishad*, *Om* is likened to a swan (*hans*), with its right eye representing righteousness (*dharma*) and left eye unrighteousness (*adharma*). The space between the eyes—equivalent to the third eye—is called the point of truth (*satya bindu*). This suggests the right side of the head is associated with positive, divine energy, while the left is not. Thus, sounds from the right side are considered spiritually significant.

The *Hatha Yoga Pradipika* (15th century), a compilation of Hatha Yoga practices, includes *Nada Anusandhan* (exploration of inner sound), which mentions listening to *Anhad Naad* from the right ear. However, it specifies that this method involves advanced practices like *pranayama, kumbhaka* (breath retention), and *rechaka* (exhalation), to balance the *ida*, *pingala*, and *sushumna* nadis (energy channels). Only then should one listen from the right ear. Crucially, it warns that attempting this without purifying these nadis can have dangerous consequences, as it affects both gross and subtle bodies. This practice is explicitly for Hatha Yogis, not householders, and requires personal guidance.

Why Focus on the *Ajna Chakra* for Householders

The "right ear" method comes from these texts but is not suited for householders practicing *Sahaj Yoga* (simple yoga) or *Surat Shabd Yoga* (yoga of sound and consciousness), which emphasize mantra chanting (*simran*) for natural focus. Saints tailored these practices for householders to progress with minimal physical or mental strain, moving from initial *Anhad Naad* sounds to higher ones like bells or flutes.

Focusing solely on the right ear in early meditation can cause issues:

- **Distraction**: Obsessing over which ear the sound comes from breaks your focus, stalling progress.
- **Physical Strain**: Forcing attention to one ear can lead to pain in the legs, back, or one side of the body, or even numbness on

one side, as you disrupt the body's energy balance.

- **Doubt**: If sounds come from the left or both ears, you may question your practice, losing confidence.

Instead, focusing on the *Ajna Chakra* is safer and more natural:

- **Natural Progression**: As you chant your mantra and focus at the third eye, your consciousness gathers from the body to this point. Initial sounds may seem to come from the left or right ear, but with practice, they center at the *Ajna Chakra*, where higher, subtler sounds (like *Om*'s hum) emerge, often from the right side, aligning with the positive energy described in scriptures.
- **Avoiding Strain**: This approach prevents physical discomfort, as you're not forcing energy to one side, allowing a smooth, balanced flow.
- **Universal Access**: Householders can practice this without the risks of advanced Hatha Yoga techniques, progressing steadily toward divine sounds.

Practical Guidance

In early *Anhad Naad Sadhana*, don't get caught up in whether sounds come from the left or right ear. These are natural variations as your consciousness adjusts. Keep your focus on the *Ajna Chakra* while chanting your mantra or listening to the sounds. As your concentration deepens, your awareness gathers to the third eye, and the sense of ears or body fades. At this stage, subtle *Anhad Naad* sounds, often from the right side, become clearer, guiding you deeper into your spiritual journey.

By sticking to this simple method, you avoid physical issues like pain or tension and progress naturally. Trust that with daily practice, divine grace will guide you from within, leading you to the higher sounds and spiritual fulfillment.

Questions and Answers

1. Should I Meditate During Brahma Muhurta (Pre-Dawn)?

Answer: Brahma Muhurta (around 4–6 AM) has benefits, like a quiet environment, but it's not mandatory. Today's busy lifestyles and responsibilities make it hard for everyone to wake up that early. If your mind isn't calm during this time or early rising disrupts your day, it's not helpful. Meditate when your mind is peaceful and you're free from time pressure—whether morning, afternoon, or evening. As you progress, every meditation session feels like Brahma Muhurta, as inner calm transcends external timing. Choose a time that suits your routine to avoid guilt or stress.

2. Should I Bathe Before Meditation?

Answer: The divine doesn't care about your physical state—only your heart's love and devotion matter. Bathing before meditation isn't necessary, but washing your face, hands, and feet can help you feel fresh and ward off sleepiness or laziness. Don't overthink this; focus on cultivating inner purity through love for the divine rather than external rituals.

3. **What If My Eyes or Pupils Keep Moving During Meditation?**

Answer: It's normal for eyes to wander initially. When you close your eyes, the eyelids drop, but subtle movements persist as your mind adjusts. To settle this, gently close your eyes twice: first, let the eyelids fall, then consciously relax them further without strain. Over time, with practice, your eyes will stabilize naturally. Don't force them to stay still, as this creates tension. Stay relaxed, and the issue will resolve itself.

4. **Should I Face East or Toward the Sun During Meditation?**

Answer: You can meditate facing any direction. Facing east (toward the sun) is fine if it resonates with you, perhaps due to reverence for the sun deity, but it's not required. The true direction for meditation is inward—toward your inner self. As you focus within, answers to all questions arise naturally. Sit in whatever direction feels peaceful to avoid unnecessary worry.

5. **Why Do I Feel Itching or Like Something Is Crawling on My Body?**

Answer: Itching or sensations like something crawling are common in early meditation because your awareness heightens, noticing subtle body signals you ignore during daily activities. These often arise when you're still, unlike in busy moments when only extreme conditions (like heat or dust) cause itching. Gently scratch the area without opening your eyes to shift your focus, then return to your practice. With time, these sensations fade as your body adjusts. They're not skin issues, so don't worry—keep meditating confidently.

6. Should I Meditate on the Floor, Bed, or Against a Wall?

Answer: Meditate wherever you're comfortable. On the floor, use a soft mat, blanket, or cushion to protect your knees from hard surfaces, preventing pain. Avoid leaning against a wall unless you have a physical condition, as it can promote slouching. Choose a setup that supports comfort and focus.

7. How Straight Should My Spine Be During Meditation?

Answer: You've likely heard the spine must be perfectly straight, but over-focusing on this can distract you. In deeper meditation, body awareness fades, so spine alignment becomes irrelevant. At the start, sit with your spine naturally straight, then relax completely—no strain or tension. Let your hands and legs rest loosely. As your consciousness rises, your spine may naturally straighten without effort, feeling pulled upward. Avoid forcing posture to prevent discomfort or discouragement.

8. How Long Should I Meditate, and How Do I Increase My Time?

Answer: Start with whatever duration feels manageable, even 15 minutes. Don't compare yourself to others who meditate for an hour—use their example as inspiration, not pressure. Sit consistently every day without moving, and your meditation time will naturally increase with practice. Focus on staying still and engaged rather than watching the clock. Over time, you'll be amazed at how hours pass without noticing, as you lose body awareness in deeper states.

9. Why Do Negative or Unwanted Thoughts Arise During Meditation?

Answer: Negative or impure thoughts come from the subconscious, especially in early meditation when your mind is still settling. Don't fear these thoughts or think they signal a mental issue. Limit exposure to stimulating content (e.g., mobile, TV, or shows which may plant suggestive ideas). Meditation, especially with *Anhad Naad* or divine sounds, gradually purifies your mind, dissolving these vices (*kaam*, *krodh*, etc.). Stay patient, avoid triggering media, and let meditation cleanse your thoughts naturally.

Understanding Kabir's Words

Many practitioners ask about Kabir's profound words: "*Jap mare, ajapa mare, anhad bhi mar jaye*" ("When chanting dies, silent chanting dies, and even *Anhad Naad* dies"). They wonder why bother with *japa* (mantra chanting) or listening to *Anhad Naad* if they all "die" in the end. Kabir's simple line captures the entire journey of meditation, from the first step to near the final destination.

Kabir's verse isn't just poetic—it's a roadmap of a meditator's spiritual journey, describing stages where practices like chanting and listening to *Anhad Naad* evolve and eventually dissolve as you reach higher states. The "death" of these practices doesn't mean they're useless; rather, they're stepping stones that lead you to transcend them. Let's explore the three stages Kabir describes, showing why each practice is vital.

Stage 1: "Jap Mare" (When Chanting Dies)

When you begin meditation, you chant a mantra (*japa*), either aloud or silently in your mind. With consistent practice, your focus on the mantra deepens, and a remarkable shift happens:

- If chanting aloud, your voice naturally falls silent without effort.
- If chanting silently, you may not even notice when the chanting stops.

At first, this might feel like a brief lapse, like dozing off, but when you resume chanting, you realize your mind was already chanting internally. This is the transition to *ajapa japa*—automatic, effortless chanting.

In this stage:

- Even during daily tasks, if you pause and check your mind, you find it chanting the mantra.
- Sitting for meditation, closing your eyes, and turning inward instantly triggers this inner chant without conscious effort.

You're no longer "doing" the chant (*japa*)—you're listening to it. Kabir calls this the "death" of deliberate chanting, as it becomes a natural, spontaneous flow. This stage shows why *japa* is essential: it trains your mind to focus, paving the way for deeper states.

Stage 2: "Ajapa Mare" (When Silent Chanting Dies)

As you meditate on the sound of *ajapa japa*, your concentration intensifies. With practice, you reach a new stage where the inner chanting (*ajapa japa*) fades, replaced by subtle sounds—the initial *Anhad Naad*. These might be:

- A whistle, cricket's chirp, or birds chirping.
- Gentle, natural sounds that mark the beginning of divine inner sounds.

Here, you're neither chanting nor listening to *ajapa japa*—you're absorbed in these *Anhad Naad* sounds. This is the "death" of *ajapa japa*, as your focus shifts to the divine sounds. Kabir highlights this progression: without *japa* leading to *ajapa japa*, you wouldn't reach *Anhad Naad*. This stage underscores the importance of listening to *Anhad Naad*, as it deepens your meditation and connects you to divine vibrations.

Stage 3: "Anhad Bhi Mar Jaye" (When Anhad Naad Dies)

As you meditate on *Anhad Naad*, the sounds evolve:

- Initially, you hear one sound, then two or three together.
- These may give way to louder sounds, like thunder, a train's rumble, or a deep roar.
- Eventually, these sounds quiet, and you hear subtler, divine sounds like *Om*, *Onkar*'s resonance, or melodies like morning prayers or *kirtan*.

By focusing on these higher *Anhad Naad* sounds, you journey inward, attaining a pure, conscious state (*shuddha chaitanya swaroop*). In this elevated state, even *Anhad Naad* ceases. This is the "death" of *Anhad Naad*, not because it's insignificant, but because you've transcended it, merging with the divine essence (*shabd*). Kabir notes this stage requires divine grace—no effort alone can take you here. Only through the blessings of your guru do you reach this point.

Why Practice Japa and Anhad Naad?

Kabir's verse might seem to dismiss *japa* and *Anhad Naad*, but it actually emphasizes their necessity. Each stage builds on the previous one:

- Without *japa*, you can't reach *ajapa japa*.
- Without *ajapa japa*, you can't access *Anhad Naad*.
- Without meditating on *Anhad Naad*, your soul (*surat*) can't merge with the divine sound (*shabd*), leading to ultimate realization.

If you doubt Kabir's words and avoid starting, you'll never reach the destination. *Japa* and *Anhad Naad* are like rungs on a ladder—each "dies" as you climb higher, but you need them to ascend. They purify your mind, deepen your focus, and prepare you for divine union.

Beyond Words: The Role of Practice

Kabir's teachings, like all saints' words, hold mysteries that can't be grasped through intellectual analysis alone. I spent a lot of time studying scriptures and saints' lives, only to find myself tangled in debates and ego-driven knowledge. It was only through meditation practice that clarity emerged. As Kabir says: *"Pothi padhi padhi jag mua, pandit bhaya na koy; dhai akhar prem ka, padhe so pandit hoy"* ("Reading books, the world dies, no one becomes wise; one who reads the two-and-a-half letters of love becomes truly wise"). Love and practice, not just study, unlock spiritual truths.

No one can fully explain these mysteries—only guru's grace grants inner understanding. *Anhad Naad* itself becomes your guide, acting as a true guru (*Satguru*), leading you through the spiritual journey. When you experience it, questions dissolve, and you're held by divine wisdom.

Don't let doubts or debates hold you back. Start your meditation practice with love and faith, regardless of the method. Whether chanting a mantra or listening to *Anhad Naad*, every moment spent remembering the divine is precious. Offer your heart to the divine (*Kul Malik*), asking for guidance. Take one step, and the divine will support you a thousandfold, opening paths and resolving doubts from within.

Avoid getting swayed by intellectual traps or overanalyzing saints' words. Meditate daily, surrendering your journey to the divine. This practice creates an inner environment where spiritual insights blossom naturally. Kabir's verse isn't a call to skip *japa* or *Anhad Naad*—it's an invitation to embrace them as vital steps toward the ultimate goal.

Coughing or Sneezing in Meditation

Some meditators notice that even without any physical issues like a cold or cough, they experience sudden intense coughing or sneezing as soon as they start focusing during meditation. Sometimes, the coughing is so strong it shakes their whole body, completely breaking their concentration. Others report coughing or burping after meditation, as if they have gas issues.

Two Reasons for Coughing or Sneezing in Meditation

These disruptions have two causes: a normal physical response and a significant spiritual process involving the balancing of *Ida* and *Pingala* nadis (energy channels). Far from being a problem, these symptoms can be a positive sign in your meditation journey. Let's dive into both causes and how to handle them.

1. Normal Cause: Sudden Shift in Consciousness

As you focus during meditation—whether on mantra chanting (*simran*), *Anhad Naad*, or your breath—your consciousness begins to gather upward, typically toward the *Ajna Chakra* (third eye). This shift causes:

- Your breathing to slow down.
- Your heart rate to decrease.

In this concentrated state, if your focus is suddenly broken—by a loud noise, a stray thought, or slight body movement—the consciousness that was gathered upward rushes back through your body in a fraction of a second. This rapid shift puts pressure on your vital energy (*prana*), breath, and heart, triggering:

- Intense coughing or sneezing.
- A jolt that may make you feel like your breath stopped (though it never does).

Some meditators, especially those whose bodies feel numb in deep focus, may panic, thinking something's wrong. **Don't worry**—this is a normal reaction to the sudden return of energy. Your breath never truly stops, no matter how deep your meditation.

How to Handle It:

- Don't get up or stop meditating when coughing or sneezing occurs.
- Stay calm, return your focus to the *Ajna Chakra*, and continue chanting your mantra or listening to *Anhad Naad*.

- With a few minutes of resumed practice, you'll settle back into focus. This issue typically fades after a few days as your body adjusts.

2. Spiritual Cause: Balancing *Ida* and *Pingala* Nadis

The second, more significant cause relates to the balancing of *Ida* (left nostril, lunar energy) and *Pingala* (right nostril, solar energy) nadis, which must align for the *Sushumna* nadi (central channel) to activate, a key step in spiritual progress. Saints call this balance "*sama hona*" (equilibrium), "*sanson ka palatna*" (breath reversal), or "*ulta chalna*" (inverse flow). Here's why it matters:

- **Normal Breathing Patterns**: Throughout the day, you breathe primarily through one nostril at a time, switching between left and right naturally. Some meditators, however, breathe mostly through one nostril, which can amplify these symptoms.
- **Nasal Blockages**: The nasal passages often have minor blockages (mucus or debris), preventing simultaneous breathing through both nostrils. In traditional Hatha Yoga, practices like *jal neti* (nasal irrigation), threading a cloth through the nose, or swallowing a strip to clear passages were used to clean these blockages and balance *Ida* and *Pingala*. These are risky for

householders without proper training and aren't necessary for most meditators.

- **Meditation's Effect**: When you enter deep focus, the intense coughing or multiple sneezes (3–4 in a row) naturally clear nasal blockages, allowing you to breathe equally through both nostrils. This is a sign that *Ida* and *Pingala* are balancing, aligning your energy for deeper meditation.

Why It's a Good Sign:

- This spontaneous balancing is a milestone, indicating your meditation is activating spiritual energy channels.
- After coughing or sneezing, you'll notice you're breathing evenly through both nostrils, and your head feels lighter, with reduced tension at the *Ajna Chakra*.
- This state allows you to re-enter deep focus quickly, often within minutes.

How to Handle It:

- **Don't Stop Meditating**: Resist the urge to get up when coughing or sneezing hits. These are temporary and signal progress.
- **Resume Focus**: After the episode, gently return your attention to the *Ajna Chakra* with your mantra or *Anhad Naad*. The balanced breathing will help you concentrate faster.
- **Optional Pranayama**: If coughing or sneezing happens repeatedly in one

session, practice gentle pranayama (natural, unforced breathing) before meditating. Avoid holding your breath (*kumbhaka*) or forcing rapid breaths, as this can strain your system. Normal, relaxed breathing is enough.

- **Trust the Process**: With daily practice, your breath will naturally flow through both nostrils during meditation, balancing *Ida* and *Pingala*. The coughing or sneezing will stop, typically within days or weeks.

Moving Forward: The Reversed Breath Sensation

As you progress beyond this stage, you might notice a subtle sensation of air or energy moving upward through your throat, as if your breath is flowing in reverse. This is what saints call "*pavan vayu ka ultana*" or "*palatna*" (reversal of the vital air). It's a natural part of spiritual awakening and nothing to fear.

How to Handle It:

- Don't focus on this sensation—it can distract you.
- Keep your attention on the *Ajna Chakra*, breathing naturally and continuing your practice (*simran* or *bhajan*).

- This feeling will also fade with time, becoming unnoticeable as your energy flow stabilizes.

These disturbances—coughing, sneezing, or reversed breath—are not setbacks but signs of progress. They show your meditation is shifting your energy upward and balancing your spiritual channels. For householders, there's no need for complex Hatha Yoga practices like *neti*—consistent, loving meditation with *simran* or *Anhad Naad* naturally achieves these results without risk.

Don't let these small hurdles discourage you. The divine (*Kul Malik, Parampita Parmeshwar*) clears every obstacle on a true meditator's path, often through unexpected guidance. Keep practicing daily with love, faith, and determination. Trust that the divine is with you at every step, ready to support your journey.

Fear in Meditation

Why fear arises during meditation, even when you're perfectly calm?

This is a critical topic for meditators, as fear can disrupt your practice if not understood.

The Four Types of Fear in Meditation

Fear in meditation can arise in four distinct stages, though not every meditator experiences all of them, as each person's mental state is unique. Here's a quick overview, with our focus on the third type:

1. **Physical Changes**: Fear from bodily sensations like jerks, increased heart rate, or worry about physical harm.
2. **Worldly Uncertainties**: Fear tied to life's challenges, like financial or personal worries.
3. **Inner Visions and Sounds**: Fear from subconscious images, voices, or sensations during meditation, which we'll explore deeply here.
4. **Ultimate Spiritual Leap**: A profound fear faced only by those nearing the highest spiritual state (*param pad*), which we'll touch on briefly.

Third Type of Fear: Inner Visions, Sounds, and Sensations

The third type of fear is the most common, affecting about 90% of meditators, and arises from experiences in the darkness behind closed eyes during meditation. These can include:

- **Visuals**: Shadows, figures moving toward you, strange faces, deceased friends or relatives, your own face, or even your meditating body as if seen from outside. Sometimes, terrifying images or your body in a distorted state appear.
- **Sounds**: Hearing your name called, familiar or unfamiliar voices urging you to stop or proceed, or extremely loud sounds, like an explosion in your head, that shake your body.
- **Sensations**: Feeling someone standing behind you, watching you, or experiencing sudden bright lights, foul odors, or pleasant fragrances.
- **Divine Experiences**: Intense divine light, brighter than anything seen with physical eyes, or powerful *Anhad Naad* sounds, like a bomb detonating, that feel overwhelming.

These experiences can be so startling that many meditators abandon their practice out of fear, mistaking them for danger or supernatural phenomena. Let's understand why they happen and how to handle them.

Why These Experiences Occur

When you meditate, you aim to calm your conscious mind, but as it quiets, your subconscious mind becomes active. This is similar to dreaming, where subconscious thoughts surface. The visions, sounds, and sensations you encounter are projections of:

- **Subconscious Impressions**: Daily experiences, especially emotionally charged ones (good, bad, or worrisome), get stored in your subconscious. Over time, or even from past lives, these impressions (*samskaras*) accumulate.
- **Mental Projections**: Like a computer screen displaying saved files when opened, your subconscious projects these stored images, voices, or feelings when your mind stills in meditation.

For example:

- Faces of deceased loved ones or strangers reflect subconscious memories, not real entities.
- Terrifying images or distorted visions of your body are mental illusions, not reality.

- Hearing your name or voices stems from subconscious thoughts, not external sources.

The Role of Darkness

When you close your eyes in meditation, you enter the darkness behind them, like a child stepping into an unknown void. This darkness can feel daunting because:

- You don't know where to go or what lies ahead.
- Your conscious mind, used to external stimuli, feels lost without a focal point.

Yet, this darkness is where spiritual treasures lie. To navigate it, you have two guides:

1. **Anhad Naad**: Divine sounds (like whistles, chirps, or *Om*) act like a voice leading you forward.
2. **Divine Light**: Even a faint glow, like a distant star, guides you toward deeper states.

Like a child holding their parents' hand, you must trust *Anhad Naad* and divine light as your "parents" in this inner journey. They lead you safely through the darkness, no matter what you see or hear.

Why Divine Experiences Cause Fear

Some meditators encounter extraordinary phenomena, like:

- **Blinding Divine Light**: A radiance so intense it feels like countless suns, filling your body with light.
- **Thunderous Anhad Naad**: Sounds so loud, like an explosion, that your body trembles, as if death is near.

These are rare, divine experiences, earned through immense spiritual merit and divine grace (*prabhu ki kripa*). Yet, many meditators fear them, mistaking them for danger, and abandon their practice. This is heartbreaking because:

- These are signs you're no ordinary meditator—you're nearing profound spiritual states.
- Such experiences are not harmful; they're transformative, connecting you to the divine.

How to Handle the Third Type of Fear

To move past these fears, adopt the mindset of a child trusting their parents, knowing the guru is with you. Here's practical guidance:

1. **Don't Engage with Visions or Sounds**:
   - Treat subconscious images (faces, shadows, or terrifying scenes) like fleeting TV scenes—observe and let them pass without focus.

- Ignore unfamiliar faces unless you see a radiant, blissful face that fills you with joy, which may be your guru. This face stands out with unmistakable peace and light.
  - Dismiss voices, even if they call your name or seem familiar. They're subconscious echoes, not real.

2. **Embrace Divine Light and Sound**:
   - If you see intense light or hear loud *Anhad Naad*, don't pull back, even if fear feels like death is near. These are divine gifts, not threats.
   - Stay calm, refocus on your mantra (*simran*) or *Anhad Naad*, and surrender to the experience. The initial jolt will pass, revealing profound peace.
   - Such moments are rare—cherish them, as they may not return for years.

3. **Surrender to Your Guru**:
   - Before meditating, seek permission from your guru, chosen deity (*isht*), or the divine (*Parampita Parmatma*), entrusting them with your protection.
   - During fear, silently call on them, reinforcing your trust. This faith is your shield, like Arjuna's trust in Krishna before his leap in the *Bhagavad Gita*.

- Complete surrender (*sampoorna vishwas*) helps you push through fear, knowing the divine is always with you (*ang sang*).

4. **Understand It's Not Real**:
   - Subconscious visions, sounds, or sensations (odors, presences) lack reality—they're mental projections, not external entities.
   - Focusing on them strengthens their recurrence, like dwelling on a computer's saved files. Ignore them, and they fade as your mind purifies.

5. **Persist Through Fear**:
   - Don't abandon meditation due to these experiences. No meditator has ever been harmed by them—fear is just your restless mind (*chanchal man*) trying to derail you.
   - If fear overwhelms, pause briefly, steady yourself, and resume meditating. Use logic (*vivek*) to override the mind's tricks.

6. **Focus on Anhad Naad and Light**:
   - In the darkness, let *Anhad Naad* (even subtle sounds like chirps) or faint divine light guide you. Don't search for a specific point or force visions—just rest in the darkness with your mantra.
   - As your focus deepens, these divine guides lead you beyond

subconscious distractions, into deeper spiritual states.

The Fourth Type of Fear: The Ultimate Leap

The fourth fear, briefly mentioned, occurs only for advanced meditators nearing *param pad* (the supreme state, like complete *samadhi*). This is the fear of total surrender, akin to facing death, where you feel pulled into a void or divine light, as if losing yourself entirely. It tests your complete trust in the divine or guru, requiring selfless love (*prem*) and longing (*virah*). Only divine grace carries you through this leap, merging your soul with the divine.

These fears—whether from subconscious visions or divine encounters—are not obstacles but signs of progress. Like a child trusting their parents in the dark, lean on *Anhad Naad* and divine light, surrendering to your guru or divine with unwavering faith. The mind may try to scare you, but no harm comes from meditation—only transformation.

Meditate daily with love and trust, seeking your guru's or divine's protection before each session. Ignore fleeting visions, embrace divine signs, and let faith guide you through the darkness. The divine (*Prabhu*) and guru are always with you, ensuring every step leads closer to your spiritual treasure.

Rising from Meditation

Every meditator focuses on how to sit for meditation, but did you know that *how you end* your meditation is just as important? If you don't transition out of meditation properly, you might face lingering physical issues that can disrupt your practice. I'll explain in a warm, practical way why these problems happen, what they feel like, and how to rise from meditation correctly to avoid them. This will help you maintain a smooth, joyful practice, especially if you're new or have been meditating for a few months.

Why Rising from Meditation Matters

When you meditate, you gather your consciousness (*chetna shakti*) from your body toward the *Ajna Chakra* (third eye), entering a deep, blissful state. Abruptly ending this state without giving your body time to readjust can cause physical discomforts, as the energy that was carefully focused returns too quickly. These issues are common but easily avoidable with the right technique.

Common Problems from Improper Rising

If you don't exit meditation gradually, you might experience:

- **Head Discomfort**: Tension, heaviness, or pulling sensations in the forehead, back, or top of the head, lasting hours after meditation.

- **Numbness or Stiffness**: Tingling, numbness, or stiffness in the legs or feet, persisting long after you stand.
- **Body Sensations**: A sudden tingling or "crawling" feeling, especially in the chest or ribs, as if energy is rushing upward.
- **Visual Disturbances**: Seeing dark spots, flashes of light, or blurred vision, making it hard to see clearly.
- **Auditory Issues (for *Anhad Naad* Practitioners)**: Sudden loud whistling sounds from the left or right, feeling like your ears are blocked or "clogged."

These issues arise solely from not transitioning out of meditation properly, not from the meditation itself. They can discourage new meditators or stall progress for those who've reached advanced states but lack guidance on this step.

Why These Problems Happen

During meditation, your practice—whether mantra chanting (*simran*), gazing (*trataka*), listening to *Anhad Naad*, breath focus, or Kundalini sadhana—aims to gather your consciousness from the body to the *Ajna Chakra*. This process:

- Starts with numbness in the feet, progressing to the legs, chest, and beyond as practice deepens.
- Eventually leaves your entire body feeling "empty," with awareness centered only at the forehead or beyond, losing all sense of physicality.

This gathering of energy takes time—often 30 minutes to an hour—to reach deep states. If you suddenly decide, "That's enough for today," and open your eyes or stand up, the consciousness that was carefully drawn upward rushes back in seconds, shocking your system. This abrupt shift causes the discomforts listed above, as your body struggles to readjust.

How to Rise from Meditation Properly

To avoid these issues, exit meditation as gradually as you entered it, giving your body time to normalize. The time needed depends on your session's length, but here's a simple, effective method:

1. **Decide to End**: When you feel ready to stop, keep your eyes closed to maintain calm.
2. **Focus on Breathing**: Shift your attention to your breath. Take 4–5 slow, deep breaths to normalize your heart rate, which slows during meditation.

3. **Move Fingers**: Gently wiggle your fingers to bring consciousness back to your hands. Continue until you feel no numbness or stiffness.
4. **Massage Face and Neck**: Lightly rub your face and neck with your hands to awaken the nerves, which may feel numb from deep focus.
5. **Open Eyes Slowly**: Gradually open your eyes to reorient to your surroundings.
6. **Move Legs**: Gently stretch or shake your legs to restore blood flow and consciousness to the lower body.
7. **Stand Up**: Rise slowly, feeling fresh and light, with no lingering discomfort.

Time Guidelines:

- For a 30-minute session, take at least 1 minute to transition.
- For 1-hour sessions, allow 2–3 minutes.
- For longer sessions (2–3 hours), 3–5 minutes may be needed initially.

With consistent practice, your body adapts, and even after hours of meditation, you'll need only seconds to transition smoothly, as your energy flow becomes naturally balanced.

Why This Works

This gradual exit allows your consciousness to redistribute evenly, preventing the shock of rapid energy return. It ensures:

- Blood flow and nerve activity normalize, avoiding numbness or tension.
- Your heart and breath stabilize, preventing sensations like tingling or heaviness.
- Your senses (vision, hearing) adjust gently, reducing flashes or ear blockages.

The Importance of Caring for Your Body

Your body is the vessel for meditation. No matter how deep your devotion or longing for the divine (*Parampita Parmatma*), physical limitations can hinder your practice. I've known meditators with intense spiritual yearning who couldn't progress because their bodies were too frail to sustain long sessions. If your body is healthy, cherish it by:

- Following this rising method to avoid strain.
- Listening to your body's needs, ensuring you meditate comfortably.
- Practicing regularly to build resilience, so your body supports deeper states.

Without a cooperative body, even the strongest spiritual desire struggles to manifest. Treat your body as a sacred tool for your journey.

These post-meditation issues are not signs of failure but of progress, showing your consciousness is shifting deeply. By rising gradually, you'll eliminate discomforts and feel refreshed after every session. This simple technique ensures your practice remains joyful and sustainable, whether you're new or advanced.Meditate with love and care, trusting that the divine (*Kul Malik*) supports every step. For *Anhad Naad* practitioners, these experiences (like sudden sounds) are part of your spiritual unfolding—embrace them with faith.

Addressing Specific Concerns

Many meditators ask about consuming non-vegetarian food, eggs, alcohol, cigarettes, onions, and garlic, and whether these affect their spiritual practice. Let's break down each topic—non-vegetarian food, eggs, alcohol, cigarettes, onions, and garlic—covering their spiritual, practical, and meditative implications.

1. Non-Vegetarian Food

Non-vegetarianism is a vast topic, but I'll summarize its key aspects:

- **Why People Eat Non-Vegetarian Food**:
    - Over 50% of non-vegetarians can't stomach raw meat, feeling nauseous at its sight. Yet, when cooked with spices, they enjoy it, driven by taste (*jeebh ka swaad*).
    - 90% can't bear watching animals (chickens, goats, fish) being slaughtered, showing their inner conscience resists the act, but taste overrides this discomfort.
    - Some only eat non-vegetarian food after drinking alcohol, unable to

consume it otherwise, further tying it to sensory indulgence.

- **Common Justifications and Their Flaws**:
    - **"It's Nature's Law"**: Some argue that animals eating animals is natural, or that not eating them would overpopulate the earth or oceans. This was debatable 100–150 years ago but is baseless today. Forests are shrinking, and wildlife is scarce. Non-vegetarian demand fuels industrial farming (poultry, goat, fish farms), not wild populations. Overfishing has depleted marine life, with strict regulations now limiting catches to protect species, as many are extinct or endangered due to massive trawling.
    - **Human Physiology**: Nature gave us teeth like herbivores (cows, goats, horses), not carnivores (dogs, lions, cats). Herbivores and humans sip water through suction, while carnivores lap it with their tongues, suggesting humans are designed for a plant-based diet.
- **Karmic Perspective**:
    - All beings fall into four categories based on their elemental composition (*panchtatva*):

1. **Sthavara** (Immobile): Plants, fruits, vegetables (only water element).
2. **Usma** (Sweat-born): Insects from dirt (air and fire elements).
3. **Andaja** (Egg-born): Birds, fish, insects (water, air, fire elements).
4. **Pindaja** (Womb-born): Mammals, including humans (earth, water, air, fire elements).

- Humans also have the fifth element, *akasha* (ether/vivek, discernment), enabling conscious choices. Eating plants (one element) incurs less karmic burden than eating animals (three or four elements), as the latter involves greater harm.
- While no action is karma-free, saints teach that minimizing karmic load eases spiritual progress and liberation from birth and death.

- **Spiritual Impact on Meditation**:
  - Non-vegetarian food, driven by taste, strengthens sensory attachments, which meditation seeks to transcend. However, meditation itself can weaken these attachments. After a year of consistent *simran* and *Anhad Naad*,

most non-vegetarians naturally reduce or quit meat, as their mind aligns with divine love.

- If you can't quit non-vegetarian food yet, don't let guilt stop you from meditating. Practice with double the effort, and your habits will shift organically.

- **Advice**:
  - If you're vegetarian, congratulations—stay committed, as it aligns with spiritual purity.
  - If you're non-vegetarian, meditate diligently without self-judgment. Gradually, your heart will guide you toward vegetarianism.
  - Avoid hating or judging non-vegetarians, as pride in vegetarianism is itself a vice. All are on their own journey.

2. Eggs

- **Debate**: Science often classifies eggs as vegetarian since they're unfertilized, but they form in a hen's womb, making them non-vegetarian in my view, despite scientific arguments. You may call me ignorant, but I see eggs as akin to animal products.

  Some people argue that even milk comes from the body so why do we consider it to be vegetarian? Well milk was designed to be consumed by their infant, egg was never designed nor intended to be consumed in any way.

- **Spiritual Impact**: Like non-vegetarian food, eggs tie to sensory indulgence, though their karmic load is lighter than meat. They don't significantly hinder meditation but may slow progress compared to a fully plant-based diet.
- **Advice**: If you eat eggs, meditate consistently. If you feel called to avoid them, follow your intuition. Choose what aligns with your spiritual goals.

3. Alcohol

- **Spiritual Impact**:
    - Alcohol directly affects the mind, as does meditation. Meditating under the influence can harm your nervous system, disrupting focus and energy flow.
    - During advanced stages, when *Ida* and *Pingala* nadis balance and *Sushumna* awakens, alcohol exacerbates issues like sudden coughing or breathlessness (*sanson ka ulta hona*), causing panic and hindering progress.
- **Advice**:

- Avoid meditating within 24 hours of drinking alcohol to protect your nervous system.
- Meditate daily, even if you drink occasionally. Over time, meditation reduces the desire for alcohol, as divine intoxication (*naam khumari*) takes over.
- Strive to minimize alcohol, aiming for the "intoxication" of *simran* and *Anhad Naad*, as Nanak says: "*Naam khumari Nanaka, chadhi rahe din raat*" (The intoxication of divine name stays day and night).

4. Cigarettes (Smoking)

- **Spiritual Impact**:
    - Smoking isn't an immediate intoxicant like alcohol, but tobacco particles linger in the blood, subtly affecting the body.
    - In advanced meditation, when *Ida* and *Pingala* balance, smokers face intensified coughing or breathlessness, making it harder to progress past this stage compared to non-smokers.
- **Advice**:
    - Try to quit smoking, as it complicates deeper meditative states.

- If you can't quit yet, meditate consistently. The practice may gradually reduce your reliance on cigarettes, as your mind seeks purer joys.
  - Saints universally discourage smoking, aligning with a sattvic lifestyle.

5. Onions and Garlic

- **Common Belief**: Onions and garlic are considered *tamasic* (promoting lethargy, anger, or lust), believed to disturb mental calm or control over desires.
- **Reality**:
  - In Hatha Yoga, yogis avoided onions and garlic because they increase *apana vayu* (downward energy), complicating breath control (*kumbhaka*), *moolbandh* (root lock), or energy retention. This is irrelevant for householders not practicing advanced pranayama.
  - Onions and garlic don't inherently disrupt meditation for householders. If you avoid them due to tradition, that's fine, but don't expect quitting them to revolutionize your spiritual life.
- **Advice**:

- Eat onions and garlic if they suit you, focusing on meditation to calm the mind.
  - If you practice Hatha Yoga with pranayama, consult a qualified teacher about dietary restrictions.
  - Avoid judging those who eat onions/garlic, as outer purity without inner transformation is incomplete.

A Householder's Diet

As a householder, don't overcomplicate your diet. The best food is simple, vegetarian, home-cooked meals suited to your body's needs. Key points:

- **Nourish Your Body**: Don't neglect eating due to spiritual zeal. A healthy body sustains long-term meditation, a lifelong journey.
- **Balance Over Obsession**: Eat enough to stay strong, avoiding extremes like fasting excessively or overeating.
- **Sattvic Focus**: Vegetarian food supports mental clarity, but meditation itself purifies deeper vices.

Broader Spiritual Perspective

- **Karma and Intention**: Per karmic principles, your intention (*mansha*) behind actions matters most. Killing unseen microbes unintentionally or a snake in self-defense incurs less karma than deliberate harm (e.g., slaughtering animals for taste). Modern solutions, like professionals relocating snakes, further reduce harm.

- **Humility Over Pride**: Vegetarianism is ideal, but it doesn't guarantee liberation (*bhava sagar par*). Pride in being vegetarian or disdain for non-vegetarians creates new vices. Saints emphasize love, humility, and meditation over diet alone.

- **Cosmetic vs. True Spirituality**: Outer rituals (avoiding certain foods) without inner transformation via meditation are superficial. Only *simran* and *Anhad Naad*, through divine grace, conquer vices like lust, anger, or attachment.

Wherever you are—vegetarian or non-vegetarian, abstaining or indulging—start meditating today. Use your discernment (*vivek*) to move toward a vegetarian, intoxicant-free life, but don't let current habits stop you. *Simran* and *Anhad Naad* will transform your desires, guiding you naturally toward purity. Your body is your vehicle, so nourish it well for this long journey. Trust the divine (*Parampita Parmatma*) to guide you through meditation. If you eat non-vegetarian food or struggle with alcohol or smoking, meditate with love and effort—change will come.

Common Nighttime Experiences in Meditation

Every meditator encounters a phase in their practice where sleep becomes restless, marked by unsettling or frightening experiences. Even those who don't notice anything unusual during meditation may face strange sensations at night. During this phase, meditators often wake suddenly at night, feeling their breath and heartbeat racing, which can spark fear and confusion. These experiences fall into two main categories: vivid dreams and physical/energetic sensations. Let's explore each, so you can recognize them if they arise.

1. Vivid, Strange Dreams

- **Unusual Settings**: Dreams of old houses, temples, or buildings, often at night.
- **Familiar Faces**: Long-forgotten friends, relatives, or deceased loved ones appear after years.
- **Unfamiliar Faces**: Strange faces you can't place or recognize.

- **Voices**: Hearing your name called repeatedly or other odd sounds, like whispers or cries.
- **Past Traumas**: Reliving painful life events or seeing terrifying faces.
- **Unfamiliar Places**: Finding yourself in unknown locations with strangers, often in distressing or sorrowful environments.

These dreams feel so vivid that they seem real, as if you're reliving those moments, which can be deeply unsettling.

2. Physical and Energetic Sensations

- **Sudden Jolts**: Feeling as if your body was violently shaken, waking you abruptly.
- **Temporary Paralysis**: Waking unable to move limbs for seconds or minutes, with your body feeling "empty" or numb.
- **Energy Movement**: Sensing something contracting or rising from your feet upward, especially in the chest or head.
- **Loud Sounds (for *Anhad Naad* Practitioners)**: Hearing an intensely loud sound, unlike anything in waking life, followed by temporary deafness as a ringing or buzzing echoes in your head.
- **Blinding Light**: Seeing dazzling light in deep sleep, so bright it feels blinding. Upon waking, the room may seem filled with light

for a few seconds, sometimes with shadowy figures visible.

- **Mystical Music**: Hearing faint, enchanting music, like distant melodies, especially in quiet nighttime silence, which can feel eerie.
- **Involuntary Movements**: Feeling your hands or feet twitch or contort against your will.
- **Floating Sensation**: Sensing a force pulling you upward, as if your body is weightless, like floating in water, unable to resist the pull.

Why These Experiences Cause Fear

Waking suddenly with a racing heart, trembling body, or inability to move can make you feel like "your soul is leaving" or something supernatural is at play. Misinformation, like tales of spirits being drawn to meditators, fuels fear. Some turn to tantriks, spending thousands without relief, as these are not occult issues but normal meditation stages. If you sit up or move abruptly during these episodes, dizziness or fainting can occur due to the rapid energy shift, heightening panic. This fear often stems from misunderstanding the root cause, leading to doubts or even abandoning meditation.

Why These Experiences Happen

These nighttime phenomena are natural outcomes of your meditation practice, particularly when your subconscious mind (*avchetan man*) activates and your consciousness (*chetna shakti*) begins to gather. Here's a breakdown of the causes:

1. Vivid Dreams: Subconscious Activation

- **Subconscious Awakening**: Consistent meditation, especially *simran* or *Anhad Naad*, activates the subconscious, where memories, emotions, and impressions (*samskaras*) from this life and past lives are stored.
- **Stored Impressions**: Dreams reflect buried thoughts—forgotten events, traumas, or faces (familiar or not). Even minor incidents from years ago can resurface vividly, feeling like they're happening now.
- **No Real Significance**: These dreams aren't prophetic or meaningful. They're subconscious "files" surfacing as your mind purifies. Focusing on them strengthens their recurrence, like replaying a saved video.

2. Physical/Energetic Sensations: Automatic Meditation in Sleep

- **Meditation Continues in Sleep**: Certain practices amplify these experiences:

- Meditating before bed.
  - Chanting mantras (*simran*) while falling asleep.
  - Focusing on *Anhad Naad* until sleep overtakes.
  - Practicing *yoga nidra* (yogic sleep).
- **How It Happens**: During these practices, your body sleeps, but your mind remains in a meditative state. Without conscious distractions, your consciousness gathers rapidly toward the *Ajna Chakra* (third eye), faster than your body is accustomed to during waking meditation.
- **Energy Surge**: This rapid gathering causes:
  - Sudden jolts, as energy shifts abruptly.
  - Loud *Anhad Naad* or blinding light, as consciousness reaches the *Ajna Chakra*.
  - Paralysis or floating sensations, as energy concentrates, leaving the body feeling "empty."
  - Involuntary movements, as energy flows through unaccustomed channels.
- **Physical Reactions**: Waking during this surge makes your body tremble, with rapid breathing and heart rate, as it struggles to adjust to the intense energy flow (*chetna shakti ka bahav*).

These experiences mirror daytime meditation phenomena (e.g., loud sounds, light) but feel more intense because they occur unconsciously in sleep, catching you off guard.

Why These Are Normal and Positive

Far from being harmful, these experiences signal progress in your meditation:

- **Subconscious Purification**: Vivid dreams show your mind is releasing old impressions, clearing mental clutter for deeper spiritual states.
- **Energy Awakening**: Physical sensations indicate your consciousness is learning to gather efficiently, a key step toward advanced stages like *Sushumna* activation or divine experiences (*Ishwar anubhav*).
- **No Supernatural Cause**: Forget myths about spirits or ghosts. These are purely internal, tied to your meditation's impact on mind and energy.

How to Handle These Experiences

To navigate this phase without fear or disruption, follow these practical steps:

1. **Don't Panic**:
    - Recognize these as normal meditation stages, not supernatural

or dangerous. No meditator has been harmed by them.
- Avoid seeking tantriks or superstitious remedies, which exploit fear and waste resources.

2. **Stay Calm During Episodes**:
   - If you wake suddenly, don't sit up or move abruptly, as the intense energy flow can cause dizziness or fainting.
   - Take 4–5 slow, deep breaths to normalize your heart rate and breathing.
   - Gently rub your head, neck, and body with your hands to redistribute consciousness (*chetna shakti*) down to your toes, restoring normal sensation.

3. **Ignore Dreams**:
   - Don't analyze or dwell on strange dreams, voices, or faces—they're subconscious projections with no real significance.
   - Focusing on them reinforces their recurrence. Treat them like passing clouds, letting them fade naturally.

4. **Adjust Your Practice if Needed**:
   - If nighttime experiences are too intense, take a short break (a few days) from meditation to let your body adjust.
   - Gradually increase daytime meditation sessions to build your

body's and mind's capacity to handle energy shifts (*chetna shakti ka simtav*). This reduces nighttime disturbances.

- o Shift meditation to earlier in the day, avoiding intense practice right before bed, especially *Anhad Naad* or *yoga nidra*.

5. **Continue with Faith**:
- o Trust that these experiences are temporary, typically lasting days or weeks as your body adapts.
- o With consistent practice, your body acclimates to energy shifts, eliminating jolts, paralysis, or loud sounds. You'll then experience only spiritual phenomena, like subtle *Anhad Naad* or divine light, during your inner journey.

6. **Surrender to the Divine**:
- o Before meditating or sleeping, seek protection from your guru, chosen deity (*isht*), or the divine (*Parampita Parmatma*), entrusting them with your safety.
- o During unsettling experiences, silently call on them, reinforcing your faith (*vishwas*). This calms fear and aligns you with divine guidance.

Moving Forward

As your practice deepens, these disturbances fade, and your body handles energy shifts effortlessly. You'll transition from subconscious purifications (dreams) and physical sensations to purely spiritual experiences, like sustained *Anhad Naad*, divine melodies, or inner light, marking progress toward higher states (*shuddha chaitanya swaroop*).

These nighttime experiences, though unsettling, are signs your meditation is working—purifying your mind and awakening your energy. They're not obstacles but stepping stones to deeper spiritual connection. Don't let fear or superstition derail you; no ghost or spirit is involved, only your own evolving consciousness.Meditate daily with love and trust, using the steps above to handle disturbances. Your body and mind will adapt, leading you to profound inner experiences. The divine (*Kul Malik*) is with you, guiding every step.

Past-Life Karma vs. Modern Science

Many meditators struggle with deep pain and distress in their worldly lives, which disrupts both their meditation practice and daily functioning. This often leads them to question whether their suffering stems from past-life karma, especially since scriptures and saints teach that our joys, sorrows, and relationships are results of past-life actions. Some are diagnosed by doctors with anxiety, depression, or overthinking, creating confusion about whether to seek psychiatric help or explore past-life regression through hypnosis at centers or ashrams. I'll explain in a grounded way why past-life regression is unreliable, how medical approaches work, and how meditation offers the truest path to healing, empowering you to navigate suffering with clarity and hope.

When facing intense suffering, meditators often seek the root cause:

- **Spiritual Perspective**: Scriptures and saints attribute life's ups and downs to past-life karma (*purva janma ke karma*). This prompts some to explore past-life regression to uncover what actions led to their current pain.

- **Medical Perspective**: Doctors, rooted in science, don't acknowledge past-life karma. They diagnose conditions like anxiety, depression, or overthinking, recommending counseling or medication, which can feel disconnected from spiritual beliefs.
- **Confusion**: Meditators feel torn between seeking a psychiatrist or trying past-life regression, unsure which path aligns with their spiritual and emotional needs.

Why Past-Life Regression Is Unreliable

Past-life regression, where a hypnotist claims to guide you to recall past-life memories, is often marketed as a way to understand your suffering. However, it's unreliable and potentially harmful for several reasons:

- **Human Limitation**: No person, without deep meditation and divine grace (*Kul Malik ki kripa*), can access past-life memories without mental disturbance. Even glimpsing pre-birth experiences in the womb could destabilize an ordinary mind, let alone past lives filled with repeated births and deaths.
- **Deceptive Nature**: Under hypnosis, your subconscious mind (*avchetan man*) projects images or stories, which may feel vivid but are often fabrications, not true memories. These sessions exploit your pain, offering false narratives that don't resolve suffering.

- **No Tangible Benefit**: I've spoken to many who underwent past-life regression. Despite claims of "knowing" past lives, their lives saw no significant spiritual or worldly transformation—only minor, fleeting changes. Spending money and time on this is wasteful, adding another layer of illusion (*maya ka chhalava*) to the mind's existing deceptions.
- **Spiritual Risk**: Seeking past-life knowledge without meditation's grounding can deepen confusion and fear, pulling you away from true spiritual progress.

How Psychiatric Treatment Works

If you consult a psychiatrist for distress labeled as depression, anxiety, or overthinking, here's what happens:

- **Initial Approach**: Doctors often prescribe sleeping pills as a temporary measure to stabilize sleep, acknowledging this isn't a cure.
- **Counseling Sessions**: The core treatment involves regular conversations between you, the doctor, and sometimes family members. Through indirect, probing questions, the psychiatrist identifies the root of your distress.
- **Five Key Areas**: Questions focus on:

1. **Financial Situation**: Are economic struggles causing stress?
2. **Relationships**: Are issues with your partner or intimacy contributing?
3. **Significant Loss**: Have you suffered a major setback (e.g., job, wealth)?
4. **Emotional Hurt**: Has betrayal, loss of a loved one, or family grief impacted you?
5. **Anger Triggers**: What provokes your strongest anger?

- **Goal**: The doctor helps you identify which of the five mental vices (*paanch vikars*)—lust (*kaam*), anger (*krodh*), greed (*lobh*), attachment (*moh*), or ego (*ahankar*)—underlies your pain. For example, grief over a brother's death points to attachment (*moh*).
- **Process**: Through counseling, the doctor guides you to mentally accept the painful reality to move forward. This acceptance depends on your mental state (*manodasha*) and can take time.
- **Limitations**: No medication can erase painful memories. Until you accept the reality, temporary aids like sleeping pills or antidepressants continue. Even the best psychiatrist can't fully heal you without your inner resolve.

The Spiritual Connection: Saints and Science Align

Interestingly, modern psychiatry unknowingly echoes the wisdom of saints, who identified the five vices as the root of all suffering centuries before medical science. As Guru Nanak said, *"Nanak dukhiya sab sansar"* (The whole world is in sorrow), because one pain replaces another until we surrender to the divine will. Both paths—psychiatric and spiritual—require accepting life's realities, but meditation offers a deeper, lasting solution by addressing the root cause: the mind's entanglement in vices.

Why Chasing Past-Life Karma Is Futile

Seeking past-life causes for current suffering is tempting but flawed:

- **No Direct Access**: Without reaching the *turiya* state (transcendental consciousness) through deep meditation, accessing past-life karma is impossible. Only divine grace, via *Anhad Naad* and divine light, allows such insight without mental collapse.
- **Focus on the Present**: Dwelling on past lives distracts from addressing present pain, which is rooted in the five vices. Identifying these (e.g., attachment to a lost loved one) is more practical and immediate.

- **Divine Will**: Saints teach that accepting the divine will transforms suffering into strength. Chasing past lives avoids this surrender, prolonging pain.

How to Heal Your Suffering

To overcome distress and restore balance in your worldly and meditative life, follow these steps:

1. **Self-Reflection**:
    - Without a psychiatrist, analyze your pain using the five vices. Ask:
        - Is financial stress (*lobh*) driving my anxiety?
        - Am I hurt by betrayal (*moh, ahankar*)?
        - Is anger (*krodh*) consuming me?
    - For example, if you're haunted by a sibling's death, recognize attachment (*moh*) as the cause. This self-awareness is the first step to healing.
2. **Daily Meditation**:
    - Practice *simran* (mantra chanting) and *Anhad Naad* meditation daily with love and devotion. This purifies the mind, weakening the five vices and fostering acceptance of life's realities.

- Before meditating, pray to the divine (*Kul Malik*) for strength to endure pain, trusting their grace to guide you.
    - Avoid meditating under the influence of sleeping pills or intoxicants, as this can harm your nervous system. If you take medication, meditate in the morning or before taking pills at night.
3. **Surrender to Divine Will**:
    - Embrace the divine's plan, accepting that all events—joy or sorrow—are part of your karmic journey. This surrender, as saints teach, is the only way to transcend suffering.
    - Offer your pain to the divine, as I do, asking for any remaining karmic debts to be fulfilled, trusting their support to carry you through.
4. **Seek Psychiatric Help if Needed**:
    - If pain feels unbearable, consult a psychiatrist for counseling and temporary medication. This can stabilize you while you work on acceptance.
    - Understand that psychiatry ultimately leads to the same truth—accepting reality—which aligns with spiritual surrender but may take longer without meditation.
5. **Avoid Past-Life Regression**:

- o Skip past-life regression sessions, as they're deceptive and offer no real resolution. Save your time and money for meditation, which reveals your true self (*asli astitva*) through divine grace.
  - o Trust that past-life karma, if relevant, will surface naturally in deep meditation (*turiya* state), guided by *Anhad Naad* and divine light, not human hypnotists.

Why Meditation Is the Ultimate Path

Saints emphasize daily meditation to control the mind's vices and face life's challenges with courage. Unlike psychiatry, which relies on external guidance, or past-life regression, which misleads, meditation:

- Directly addresses the five vices, purifying your mind.
- Builds inner strength (*shakti*) to accept and transcend suffering.
- Connects you to the divine (*Parampita Parmatma*), revealing your true essence and purpose.
- Prepares you to handle even the greatest adversities (*vipada*) with gratitude (*shukr*) and resilience.

In deep meditation, you may glimpse past-life insights, but only with divine grace and proper grounding. This state lifts the "veil of darkness" (*andhkar ki chadar*), inspiring complete surrender to the divine, far beyond what hypnosis can offer.

Your pain, though heavy, is a call to deepen your spiritual practice. Don't chase past-life answers or fear medical labels like depression. Instead, meditate daily with *simran* and *Anhad Naad*, reflecting on the five vices to uncover your pain's roots. Surrender to the divine will, trusting that every sorrow is part of your journey to liberation. If suffering overwhelms, a psychiatrist can help, but know that true healing lies in accepting the divine's plan through meditation. Avoid past-life regression—it's a distraction from your real work. The divine (*Kul Malik*) is with you, offering strength through every trial. As Nanak said, only by wearing the "cloak of divine will" can we endure life's sorrows. Keep meditating with love, and your path will shine brighter.

Why You Cry During Spiritual Practices

Many meditators notice an unexpected urge to cry or feel a wave of sadness during spiritual practices like meditation, worship, listening to devotional music, attending *satsang*, or visiting sacred places. Some even burst into tears during meditation, leading to confusion or worry. Doctors may label this as anxiety or depression, but it's actually a profound and positive stage of meditation called *chitta shuddhi* (purification of the mind).

This emotional response—tears, sadness, or an urge to cry—arises when your mind and heart connect deeply with the divine during spiritual activities. It's not a sign of weakness or illness but a natural part of your spiritual journey. Let's break it down:

The Role of the Mind and Emotions

- **Worldly Emotions**: In daily life, your mind (*man*) is shaped by emotions tied to love, sacrifice, and pain. For example:
    - A mother's love drives her to protect her child from even the slightest

discomfort, enduring hardships silently.

- A father sacrifices greatly for his family, hiding his pain to appear strong.
- A daughter-in-law conceals her struggles in her new home to maintain harmony.
- Parents continue loving their children, even when unappreciated or forgotten.

- **Suppressed Pain**: When your love or sacrifices go unreciprocated—when others don't value your emotions—you feel deep hurt. Yet, societal norms (*lok-laj*) or love compel you to suppress this pain, never letting a tear fall in front of others. These unexpressed emotions—grief, betrayal, or longing—sink into your subconscious mind (*avchetan man*), creating an inner restlessness.

The Spiritual Trigger

- **Moments of Connection**: During meditation (*simran*), worship, *satsang*, devotional music, or visits to sacred places, your focus shifts inward. As your emotions align with the divine words or atmosphere, your mind becomes still, and you feel a profound solitude, even amidst a crowd.

- **Release of Emotions**: In this stillness, the subconscious releases its buried pain. The love, longing, or unexpressed grief you've held back surfaces, and tears flow naturally. This is why you cry without an apparent reason—it's your heart responding to the divine presence.
- **Divine Proximity**: As you feel closer to the divine (*Kul Malik, Parampita Parmatma*), who embodies infinite love, compassion, and mercy, your heart overflows. The divine's presence stirs your soul, melting the barriers of suppressed emotions.

The Stages of This Experience

This emotional phase unfolds progressively in meditation:

1. **Initial Tears**: Early in practice, as you achieve slight focus (*ekagrata*) through *simran*, tears well up without reason, like a gentle release.
2. **Sadness and Urge to Cry**: With deeper focus, your mind feels a tender sadness (*udasi*), and you strongly desire to cry, unable to hold back tears.
3. **Uncontrollable Weeping**: In profound moments, you may sob openly (*phoot-phoot kar rona*), especially during *Anhad Naad* or divine experiences, as your heart surrenders to the divine.

4. **Profound Peace**: After crying, you feel immense peace (*aseem shanti*), as if a weight has lifted, leaving your mind clearer and lighter.

Why This Is a Positive Stage

Far from being a problem, crying during spiritual practices is a sacred milestone known as:

- **Chitta Shuddhi**: Vedanta and Upanishads describe this as purification of the mind (*chitta*), where emotional impurities are cleansed through tears.
- **Man ka Nirmal Hona**: Saints call it the mind becoming pure (*nirmal*), a prerequisite for realizing the ultimate truth (*Paramtattva*).

This stage signifies:

- **Purification**: Tears wash away mental vices (*vikars*) like attachment (*moh*), anger (*krodh*), or ego (*ahankar*), accumulated from worldly experiences.
- **Divine Love**: Your growing love for the divine (*Ishwar ke prati prem*) softens your heart, making it receptive to forgiveness, compassion, and universal love.
- **Clarity and Purpose**: As your mind purifies, you gain clarity to prioritize your spiritual goal (*Ishwar prapti*) over worldly chaos, setting meaningful life priorities.

Why It's Not Anxiety or Depression

Doctors may misinterpret this as anxiety or depression because modern science views emotional outbursts through a clinical lens. However:

- These tears come from a spiritual connection, not distress. They're not triggered by sadness or fear but by love, longing, or divine presence.
- Unlike depression's persistent heaviness, this crying brings relief and peace, marking it as a healing process.
- It's a temporary phase, fading as your mind purifies, unlike chronic mental health issues requiring ongoing treatment.

Visiting a doctor isn't necessary unless you feel persistently distressed outside spiritual practices. This is a spiritual stage, not a medical condition.

How to Embrace This Stage

To fully benefit from this purifying phase and avoid confusion, follow these steps:

1. **Don't Suppress Tears**:

- o Let tears flow freely during meditation, *simran*, or *satsang*. Suppressing them halts purification, as tears release subconscious pain and vices.
  - o The more you allow this release, the lighter your mind and the deeper your meditation becomes.
2. **Surrender to the Divine**:
   - o Before meditating or engaging in spiritual activities, pray to your guru, deity (*ishta*), or *Parampita Parmatma* for guidance, offering your heart to them.
   - o During tears, silently call on divine love, trusting this phase is their grace (*kripa*) cleansing your soul.
3. **Don't Fear Sadness**:
   - o The sadness you feel isn't despair but a tender longing (*viraha*) for the divine, like a child yearning for a parent. Embrace it as a sign of growing devotion.
   - o Recognize that this sadness passes, leaving peace and joy in its wake.
4. **Stay Consistent**:
   - o Meditate daily with love and faith, practicing *simran* or *Anhad Naad* to deepen focus. Consistency strengthens this purification, preparing you for higher spiritual experiences.

- Attend *satsang*, serve saints (*sadhu seva*), or listen to spiritual discourses, as these amplify divine connection that triggers purification.

5. **Let Go of Ego**:
   - Don't let pride (*ahankar*) or shame stop you from crying, even if it feels vulnerable. As a mother feeds her child only when they cries, the divine responds to your heartfelt tears (*prem bhara rona*).
   - Surrender your ego, trusting the divine will never abandon you, even in life's greatest trials.

6. **Avoid Overthinking**:
   - Don't analyze why you're crying or label it as weakness. It's a natural part of *chitta shuddhi*, not a flaw.
   - Focus on the peace that follows, reinforcing your commitment to meditation.

The Deeper Spiritual Significance

This stage reflects your soul's awakening:

- **Divine Intimacy**: Tears flow because you're nearing the divine, whose love is an ocean (*prem, karuna, daya ka samandar*). Your heart can't stay dry in their presence.
- **Forgiveness and Love**: As vices dissolve, you gain the strength to forgive others and

love unconditionally, aligning with the divine's qualities.

- **Life's Purpose**: You see beyond worldly pursuits (*bhagdaud, maramari*), prioritizing liberation (*Ishwar prapti*) as your ultimate goal.

Saints urge *sadh sangat* (company of the wise) and service because they loosen the grip of mind and illusion (*man aur maya*), sparking curiosity for truth (*satya ki jigyaasa*). Your tears are a sign this process is unfolding.

A Heartfelt Metaphor

Think of yourself as a child crying for their mother. A mother, who loves her child more than life, feeds them only when they cry. Similarly, don't let ego stop you from crying before the divine (*Kul Malik*). Your tears, filled with love, draw their grace, ensuring you're never alone, even in life's darkest moments. As you persist in meditation, this phase evolves. Your tears will transform into a deeper longing (*tadap*), where every breath and pore (*rom-rom*) yearns for the divine, like a fish out of water. This prepares you to uphold your guru's teachings, even at great sacrifice, with unwavering faith. The divine's presence (*ang sang*) becomes your constant companion.

Your tears are not a sign of illness but a sacred gift of *chitta shuddhi*, purifying your mind for divine union. Don't fear or suppress them—let them flow, trusting they're washing away pain and vices. Meditate daily with *simran* and *Anhad Naad*, surrender to the divine, and stay in *sadh sangat* to deepen this cleansing. Forget worldly judgments that call emotional surrender foolish. Your goal is *Ishwar prapti*, and these tears are steps toward it. Train your mind to stop dwelling on petty sorrows, preparing for the divine love that will consume you. The divine (*Parampita Parmatma*) is with you, guiding every tear and breath.

Understanding Popular Meditation Practices

Many meditators, especially newcomers and even seasoned practitioners, come across various meditation practices like Twin Flame Meditation, Transcendental Meditation, Music Meditation for chakra activation, Third Eye opening, Past Life Regression, or Tantra Sadhana. These can be confusing due to their compelling presentations, leaving you unsure about their authenticity or value. I'll explain in a clear way what these practices entail, why some are misleading, and why saints focus on authentic meditation rooted in *simran* and *Anhad Naad*.

Let's explore the mentioned practices, their claims, and their spiritual validity, so you can make informed choices.

1. Twin Flame Meditation

- **What It Is**: This practice claims that your soul, unable to incarnate in one body, splits into two, creating two individuals with the same soul in different bodies. These "twin flames" are drawn to each other through life's trials, supposedly to practice meditation together for spiritual union.

- **Reality**: Despite its romantic appeal, 99.9% of Twin Flame Meditation revolves around physical attraction, sexual desire (*kaam*), and emotional attachment, not spirituality. It's often a business-driven concept exploiting youthful curiosity.
- **Why It's Misleading**:
    - Each soul is unique, with distinct karma from past lives, making the "split soul" theory baseless. Souls connect through karmic bonds, not shared essence.
    - The only true love worthy of pursuit is for the divine (*Kul Malik*) and the guru who guides you there. Seeking spirituality in another person risks amplifying mental vices (*vikars*) like lust or attachment.
    - If your "twin flame" is entangled in vices, this practice can deepen your own, pulling you away from true meditation.
- **Advice**: Avoid Twin Flame Meditation. Focus on *simran* and *Anhad Naad* to cultivate divine love, which transcends worldly relationships.

2. Transcendental Meditation

- **What It Is**: Popularized in the West, this involves chanting a personalized mantra (e.g., linked to a sound like a flute if you love flutes) to calm the mind and reduce stress.
- **Reality**: It's a diluted imitation of *simran* or *Anhad Naad* taught by saints and gurus. Western practitioners sought mental peace, not spiritual awakening, so the practice lacks depth.
- **Why It's Limited**:
    - Its mantras are chosen based on personal preferences, not divine potency, missing the transformative power of guru-given mantras.
    - It focuses on temporary mental relief, not liberation (*moksha*) or divine connection (*Ishwar prapti*).
    - Saints have already given us profound *simran* practices, making Transcendental Meditation redundant.
- **Advice**: Stick to *simran* as taught by gurus, which leads to true spiritual progress, rather than chasing a shallow alternative.

3. Music Meditation (Chakra Activation, Third Eye Opening)

- **What It Is**: This involves listening to specific music or frequencies claimed to awaken chakras, activate energy, or open the Third Eye (*Ajna Chakra*). Some tracks are sold for thousands of rupees with promises of instant spiritual awakening.
- **Reality**: Inspired by the concept of *Anhad Naad* (divine inner sound), these are commercialized external sounds lacking spiritual potency. Foreign companies, learning from Indian saints, now market these to Indians as "spiritual tools."
- **Why It's Misleading**:
    - No external music can awaken chakras or the Third Eye. These are inner processes activated through disciplined *simran* and *Anhad Naad* meditation under divine grace.
    - External music may relax you temporarily, easing stress or helping focus when you're new to meditation. However, it can't advance you spiritually beyond initial comfort.
    - If machine-made music feels soothing, imagine the bliss of *Anhad Naad*—divine inner sound that makes every pore (*rom-rom*) dance with joy.
    - It's disheartening that even Indians, steeped in spiritual traditions, fall for

these costly gimmicks instead of trusting authentic practices.

- **Advice**: Use calming music briefly as a beginner to settle your mind, then shift to *Anhad Naad* meditation. Don't waste money on music claiming to open chakras or the Third Eye—true awakening comes from within.

4. Past Life Regression

- **What It Is**: A form of hypnosis (*sammohan*) where a practitioner claims to guide you to recall past-life memories, often to explain current suffering as a result of past karma.
- **Reality**: It's not a meditation practice but a psychological manipulation. Hypnosis surfaces subconscious projections, not actual past-life events, offering no real spiritual benefit.
- **Why It's Futile**:
    - Past-life knowledge requires deep meditation (*turiya* state) and divine grace, not external hypnosis. Without this, such insights can destabilize the mind.
    - Suffering stems from present mental vices (*kaam, krodh, lobh, moh,*

ahankar), not past lives, which can't be altered.
  - Practitioners exploit emotional pain, offering false narratives that don't resolve issues, as discussed in my previous response on past-life regression.
- **Advice**: Focus on healing present pain through *simran* and *Anhad Naad*. Past-life insights, if needed, will arise naturally in deep meditation, guided by the divine.

5. Tantra Sadhana

- **What It Is**: Practices aimed at activating lower chakras (e.g., *Muladhara*, *Svadhisthana*) or harnessing energies, often involving rituals, mantras, or visualizations, sometimes linked to occult or mystical powers.
- **Reality**: While some tantric practices have historical roots, most modern versions are diluted or sensationalized, focusing on lower chakras where illusion (*maya*) dominates.
- **Why It's Risky**:
  - Saints teach focusing on the Third Eye during *simran* to transcend *maya*. Lower chakras are entangled in mental vices, amplifying desires (e.g., lust, greed) if targeted.
  - Meditating on lower chakras can manifest your dominant vice (e.g.,

lust appears as temptation), deceiving the mind and stalling progress.

- o Practitioners may become stuck in *tantrik* rituals or occult pursuits (e.g., *jhad-phoonk*), unable to advance spiritually.
- o True liberation comes from purifying the mind through *Anhad Naad* and divine light (*divya prakash*), not external rituals.
- **Advice**: Avoid tantra sadhana unless guided by an authentic guru. Practice *simran* with focus on the Third Eye to safely transcend vices and *maya*.

Why These Practices Cause Confusion

- **Compelling Marketing**: YouTube videos present these practices with persuasive flair, blending spiritual buzzwords (e.g., "Third Eye," "chakras") with promises of quick results, attracting both new and experienced meditators.
- **Western Influence**: Many practices originate abroad, appealing to youth who view foreign concepts as novel or superior, despite their lack of spiritual depth compared to Indian traditions.

- **Lack of Foundation**: Unlike *simran* and *Anhad Naad*, rooted in saints' teachings, these practices often lack a clear spiritual lineage or goal, offering temporary effects at best.
- **Distraction from Truth**: Chasing trendy meditations diverts you from the simple, profound path of daily *simran*, which leads to divine union (*Ishwar prapti*).

The True Path: Simran and Anhad Naad

Saints and gurus teach a simple, profound path to transcend mind and illusion (*man aur maya*):

- **Daily Practice**: Practice *simran* (mantra chanting) and *Anhad Naad* (divine inner sound) with love and faith, focusing on the Third Eye.
- **Purpose**: Purify the mind, overcome vices (*kaam, krodh, lobh, moh, ahankar*), and realize the divine (*Kul Malik*).
- **Why It Works**:
    - Unlike external music or hypnosis, *Anhad Naad* is the divine sound within, awakening your soul (*rom-rom khil jata hai*).
    - Unlike lower chakra practices, focusing on the Third Eye bypasses

> _maya_'s deceptions, ensuring safe progress.
>   ○ It's a direct path to liberation, not a shortcut or cosmetic spirituality (_cosmetic spirituality_).
> - **No Shortcuts**: Spiritual awakening (_Ishwar prapti_) requires consistent effort, not trendy practices promising instant results.

Don't be swayed by flashy meditations—Twin Flame, Transcendental, Music, Past Life Regression, or Tantra Sadhana. They're often shallow, deceptive, or risky, pulling you from the true path. Trust the timeless wisdom of saints: practice _simran_ and _Anhad Naad_ daily, focusing on the Third Eye, to transcend _maya_ and embrace divine love (_Ishwar prem_).

Anhad Naad meditation is a simple yet profound practice with two steps: first, chanting a mantra (_simran_) while seated in a meditation posture, and second, stopping the chanting to focus entirely on the inner divine sound (_Anhad Naad_). However, meditators often have questions about how to navigate this practice effectively, especially when the inner sound becomes prominent or time constraints arise.

The Three Questions Addressed

1. If *Anhad Naad* is heard constantly, can I skip *simran* and focus directly on the sound?
2. How do I decide when to stop *simran* and focus on *Anhad Naad* during meditation?
3. What if I can't complete the guru-prescribed two hours of *simran* daily?

Let's dive into each, ensuring you understand the practice and its nuances.

1. Should You Skip Simran if Anhad Naad Is Constantly Audible?

Some meditators notice that even with slight calmness, they hear *Anhad Naad* sounds (e.g., a hum, crickets, or birds chirping) all the time, not just during meditation. They wonder if they can bypass *simran* and focus directly on the sound when meditating. Here's why *simran* remains crucial:

- **The Challenge of Direct Focus**:
  - Focusing solely on *Anhad Naad* without *simran* may work for a few minutes, but thoughts inevitably intrude, pulling your attention outward. You may not notice this drift until later, wasting your meditation time in a cycle of distraction and refocusing.
  - This struggle leads to frustration or self-doubt (*aatmaglani*), as you feel you're not meditating effectively despite effort, robbing you of peace (*shanti*) and joy (*anand*).
- **The Role of Simran**:
  - *Simran* anchors your restless mind (*chanchal man*), preventing it from wandering. Saints emphasize *simran*—even while walking or breathing (*swaas-swaas simran*)—to achieve *ajapa jap* (automatic mantra repetition).
  - With regular *simran* practice, your mind chants the mantra internally, even when you're not consciously trying. This happens naturally, like hearing *Anhad Naad* when calm. For example, closing your eyes and observing your mind reveals it chanting the mantra effortlessly.
- **Why Simran Before Anhad Naad**:

- Starting with *simran* builds focus (*ekagrata*), preparing your mind to stay centered on *Anhad Naad*. When you stop chanting, your mind continues *simran* subtly, acting like an anchor (as a small anchor holds a large ship), keeping distractions at bay.
    - If your attention drifts from *Anhad Naad*, the underlying *ajapa jap* pulls you back, ensuring sustained meditation.
- **Advice**:
    - Don't skip *simran*, even if *Anhad Naad* is constant. Begin every session with focused *simran* to stabilize your mind, then shift to *Anhad Naad*.
    - Over time, *ajapa jap* and *Anhad Naad* merge, allowing you to hear subtler divine sounds (*sukshma dhun*), deepening your practice.

2. How to Decide When to Stop Simran and Focus on Anhad Naad?

New meditators often struggle with timing the transition from *simran* to *Anhad Naad*. Here's a practical guide to make this shift seamless:

- **Step-by-Step Process**:

- **Start with Simran**: Sit in your meditation posture and chant your mantra mentally with full focus. You may hear *Anhad Naad* faintly in the background, but ignore it initially. Keep chanting until your body and mind feel calm and external thoughts (*bahari vichar*) diminish, typically after 30–40 minutes for beginners.
  - **Transition to Anhad Naad**: When you sense inner stillness (e.g., fewer thoughts, relaxed body), stop *simran* and focus entirely on the inner sound. Imagine tracing the sound to its source (*jad*), as if seeking its origin, to deepen concentration.
  - **Handle Distractions**: If thoughts resurface after a few minutes, resume *simran* for 2–3 minutes while also listening to *Anhad Naad*. This dual focus quickly restores your previous stillness, often faster than the initial *simran* phase.
  - **Refine the Practice**: Over time, your mind learns to shift effortlessly from *simran* to *Anhad Naad*. You may not even notice when *simran* stops, as your focus merges with the sound's rhythm (*lay*), creating a flow state.
- **Practical Example**:

- If you meditate for one hour, dedicate 45 minutes to *simran* and 15–20 minutes to *Anhad Naad*. Use earplugs (e.g., foam earbuds) during the *Anhad Naad* phase to block external noise and enhance inner sound clarity.
  - If distractions return, chant the mantra briefly while listening to the sound, then resume *Anhad Naad* focus.
- **Why This Works**:
  - *Simran* builds the focus needed for *Anhad Naad*, which requires a calm, centered mind. Alternating between the two ensures sustained concentration, preventing wasted sessions.
  - Regular practice makes the transition automatic, reducing the time needed for *simran* as your mind attunes to *Anhad Naad*.
- **Advice**:
  - Don't rush to stop *simran*. Wait for inner calm, then shift to *Anhad Naad*. If distracted, briefly resume *simran* alongside listening. Practice daily to make this flow natural.

3. What If You Can't Complete Two Hours of Simran Daily?

Some meditators, per their guru's initiation (*diiksha*), are instructed to practice two hours of *simran* daily but struggle to meet this requirement due to time constraints or other responsibilities. They wonder how to incorporate *Anhad Naad*. Here's how to approach this:

- **The Power of Anhad Naad**:
    - *Anhad Naad* is the divine force (*shakti*) that enables prolonged meditation without physical strain. Without it, sitting still for hours is nearly impossible, as the body lacks the energy to remain steady.
    - *Anhad Naad* gathers consciousness (*chetna shakti*) from the body to the mind, a process that *simran* alone achieves slowly and requires years of practice.
- **Practical Solution**:
    - If you can only manage one hour of *simran*, don't stop there, thinking you've failed to meet the two-hour goal. Always dedicate time to *Anhad Naad* in the same session.
    - For example, in a one-hour session, spend 45 minutes on *simran* and 15 minutes on *Anhad Naad*. Treat the initial *Anhad Naad* sound you hear (e.g., hum, crickets) as the divine voice (*Parmatma ki awaaz*) and

listen with full devotion (*prem* and *ekagrata*).

- Use earplugs to enhance focus on the sound, helping you stay immersed.

- **Why Include Anhad Naad**:
  - Even brief *Anhad Naad* practice infuses your body with energy (*urja*), alleviating physical issues (e.g., fatigue, restlessness) that hinder long meditation.
  - This energy enables you to gradually extend your *simran* time, eventually meeting the two-hour goal with ease.
  - *Anhad Naad* accelerates spiritual progress, leading to the ultimate meditative state (*param avastha*) more efficiently than *simran* alone.
- **Long-Term Perspective**:
  - As you progress, *Anhad Naad's* subtler sounds (*sukshma dhun*) become audible, requiring less *simran*. For example, two hours of *simran* once needed for deep focus may be achieved in just two minutes, as *Anhad Naad's* magnetic pull (*kheench*) draws your mind inward instantly.
  - However, reaching this stage requires daily practice of both *simran* and *Anhad Naad* to condition your body and mind.

- **Advice**:
    - ○ If you can't do two hours of *simran*, practice what you can (e.g., one hour), but always include *Anhad Naad* time. Start with *simran*, then listen to the divine sound with devotion. This builds the energy to extend your practice and fulfill your guru's guidance.
    - ○

Additional Insight: Preparing for Advanced Stages

Some meditators experience sudden, intense focus in *Anhad Naad*, where the sound's power overwhelms their body and mind, causing fear or panic (*ghabrahat*). This happens when the body isn't accustomed to the rapid inward pull of consciousness. To avoid this:

- Practice consistently every day, combining *simran* and *Anhad Naad*. This gradually trains your body to handle energy shifts, making deep meditation effortless (*makkhan se baal kheenchana*—like pulling a hair from butter).
- Trust the divine (*Kul Malik, Parampita Parmatma*) during practice, surrendering fears to their guidance.

With regular practice, entering deep meditative states becomes natural, and you'll access subtler *Anhad Naad* sounds without discomfort, marking significant spiritual growth.

The Three Stages of Anhad Naad

To clarify the practice's progression:

1. **Initial Stage**: You consciously practice *jap* (deliberate mantra chanting) and hear basic *Anhad Naad* sounds (e.g., hum, crickets). *Simran* is essential to build focus.
2. **Ajapa Jap Stage**: With daily practice, your mind chants the mantra automatically (*ajapa jap*), anchoring attention. You hear *Anhad Naad* clearly, and *simran* supports sustained focus.
3. **Subtle Stage**: *Anhad Naad*'s finer sounds (*sukshma dhun*) emerge, requiring minimal *simran*. Your mind merges effortlessly with the divine sound, leading to higher states.

Each stage builds on daily *simran* and *Anhad Naad* practice, ensuring steady progress.

Anhad Naad meditation is a divine gift, simple yet transformative. Don't skip *simran*—it's the anchor that steadies your mind for *Anhad Naad*'s depths. Start with focused chanting, shift to the divine sound when calm, and return to *simran* if distracted. Even if you can't meet two hours of *simran*, include *Anhad Naad* daily to build energy and progress.

Trust the process, practicing with love and devotion (*prem* and *shraddha*). The divine (*Parampita Parmatma*) is with you, guiding every sound and breath. As saints teach, *simran* and *Anhad Naad* lead to *Ishwar prapti*. Keep meditating daily, and your heart will sing with divine joy (*rom-rom khil jata hai*).

Why Thoughts Arise in Meditation

One of the biggest hurdles for meditators is the flood of unwanted thoughts that disrupt focus during meditation. Despite their love for meditation and awareness of its benefits, these relentless thoughts prevent concentration (*ekagrata*), leading to frustration and discouragement. I'll share two powerful, time-tested techniques to manage these thoughts, tailored for beginners and those practicing mantra-based *simran* as guided by their guru. I'll explain why thoughts arise, how these methods work, and how they lead to deeper meditation, empowering you to overcome this obstacle with confidence and joy.

To tackle thoughts effectively, it's essential to understand their nature:

- **The Mind's Habit**: From birth, your mind (*man*) is conditioned to focus outward through sensory experiences—sights, sounds, words, and life's highs and lows. These form a vast storehouse (*bhandar*) of memories and impressions in your subconscious (*avchetan man*).

- **Constant Activity**: The mind is restless, incessantly generating thoughts, even when you don't want it to. This is its default state (*nomal avastha*), like a machine that never stops.
- **Meditation's Challenge**: When you meditate, you aim to either silence these thoughts or focus solely on your mantra (*simran*). However, the mantra itself is a thought, so what's the difference between it and worldly thoughts?
  - **Worldly Thoughts**: These are chaotic, jumping from one topic (e.g., a friend) to another (e.g., work, past events) without you noticing, taking your mind "across seven seas" while you sit still.
  - **Mantra Thoughts**: A mantra is a single, deliberate thought repeated consistently. Even if other thoughts arise, they often align with divine feelings (*Ishwar anubhuti*) or your guru's guidance, keeping you spiritually anchored.
- **The Goal**: Meditation trains the mind to pause its outward rush and rest inward, either in silence or on the mantra, breaking the cycle of scattered thoughts.

Without understanding this, no technique will fully work. Now, let's explore two methods to control thoughts, one for beginners and one for *simran* practitioners.

Method 1: For Beginners (New to Meditation)

This technique is perfect for those who've started meditating recently (days or months) and struggle with a storm of thoughts. It trains the mind to pause and creates moments of stillness.

- **How to Practice**:
    - **Settle In**: Sit in your meditation posture (*asana*), ensuring comfort. Begin with a heartfelt prayer to the divine (*Ishwar*), asking them to accept your meditation (*bhakti* and *ardaas*) and guide you.
    - **Ask the Mind a Question**: Silently, in your mind, ask, "What will be the next thought in my mind?" (*Mere man mein aane wala agla vichar kya hoga?*)
    - **Wait and Observe**: Pause for a few seconds, observing what thought arises. If no thought comes, you'll experience a brief moment of mental stillness as the mind waits for the "next thought."
    - **Repeat**: After a few seconds, ask the same question again, "What will be the next thought?" Continue this

cycle multiple times during your session.

- ○ **Stay Patient**: Initially, thoughts may still arise, but the gaps of stillness will grow longer with practice.
- **Why It Works**:
  - ○ Asking "What's next?" interrupts the mind's automatic thought chain, forcing it to pause and listen inward, a state it's unaccustomed to.
  - ○ These fleeting seconds of stillness are the essence of meditation, countering the mind's habit of endlessly producing thoughts from its storehouse.
  - ○ Over time, the mind learns to rest inward (*andar rukna*), reducing thought frequency and building focus.
- **Benefits**:
  - ○ Creates moments of mental emptiness (*khaali rehna*), essential for deeper meditation.
  - ○ Reduces frustration by giving you control over the thought process.
  - ○ Builds confidence as you experience brief, thought-free states.

- **Advice**:

- ○ Practice this daily during meditation. Start with 5–10 minutes, gradually increasing as you feel comfortable.
- ○ This is ideal for beginners, as it requires no prior mantra or guru initiation, making it accessible yet effective.

Method 2: For Simran Practitioners (With Guru-Given Mantra)

This technique is for meditators who practice *simran* or mantra chanting (*jap*) as guided by their guru. It leverages the mantra to anchor the mind and deepen focus, even amidst distractions.

- **The Problem**: During *simran*, the mind initially focuses on the mantra for a few seconds but soon wanders to unrelated thoughts (e.g., work, family), pulling you away without you realizing.
- **How to Practice**:
  - ○ **Settle and Pray**: Sit in your meditation posture, pray to the divine for guidance, and surrender your practice to them.
  - ○ **Focus on Inner Darkness**: Close your eyes and gaze into the darkness behind them, as if looking at a blank screen. Don't search for anything or try to "see"

something—just rest your attention in this dark space.

- **Rapid Mantra Chanting**: Chant your mantra mentally at a fast pace, creating a continuous rhythm (*dhun*). For example, instead of "Ram... Ram... Ram" with gaps, chant "RamRamRamRam" without pauses, like a flowing melody.
  - Maintain this speed for a few minutes, keeping your gaze in the inner darkness.
- **Listen to the Mantra**: As you chant rapidly, notice that the mantra starts "echoing" internally—you're not just chanting but hearing it within. This shift happens naturally within seconds.
- **Let Vision Fade**: With sustained chanting, your eyes stop "seeing" the darkness, and your mind merges fully with the mantra, blocking out other thoughts.
- **Why It Works**:
  - Rapid chanting eliminates gaps between mantra repetitions, which are windows for stray thoughts to creep in. The continuous rhythm occupies the mind, leaving no room for distractions.

- Focusing on inner darkness anchors attention inward, reducing external sensory pull.
  - Hearing the mantra internally (*antar sunai dena*) aligns the mind with divine vibration, fostering *ekagrata* and spiritual connection (*Ishwar anubhuti*).
  - This mirrors *simran*'s progression toward *ajapa jap* (automatic chanting), where the mantra flows effortlessly.
- **Benefits**:
  - Quickly controls wandering thoughts, keeping the mind on the mantra.
  - Deepens *simran*, leading to peace (*shanti*) and joy (*anand*).
  - Prepares you for *Anhad Naad* or higher meditative states by stabilizing focus.
- **Advice**:
  - Practice this during your *simran* sessions, starting with 5–10 minutes of rapid chanting, then slowing down as focus strengthens.
  - If thoughts persist, return to the fast rhythm briefly to reset. Combine with *Anhad Naad* listening if guided by your guru.

How These Methods Transform Your Practice

- **Short-Term**: Both methods reduce thought frequency within days, giving you moments of stillness (Method 1) or mantra-focused flow (Method 2). You'll feel less frustrated and more motivated to meditate daily.
- **Long-Term**: With consistent practice, the mind becomes naturally still (*sahaj avastha*), staying inward during meditation. This leads to:
    - Deeper concentration (*ekagrata*), enabling progress to advanced stages like *Anhad Naad* or divine experiences (*Ishwar anubhuti*).
    - Inner joy (*anand*), as the mind itself urges you to meditate, replacing discouragement with enthusiasm.
    - Control over mental vices (*vikars*), as thoughts align with divine love (*prem*) rather than worldly chaos.

A Nod to Tradition

These methods align with ancient wisdom. Adi Shankaracharya, India's great meditation scientist (*dhyan vaigyanik*), taught similar techniques to free the mind from thoughts, as per Vedanta and Upanishads.

Thoughts during meditation are normal, not a failure—they're just the mind's habit of wandering.

Whether you're a beginner or a *simran* practitioner, these two methods—questioning the mind or rapid mantra chanting—will quiet the storm of thoughts, bringing peace and focus.

Start today: try Method 1 if you're new, or Method 2 if you practice *simran*. Pray to the divine (*Kul Malik*) before each session, trusting their grace to guide you. Your love for meditation is your strength—let it shine through daily practice. Soon, your mind will rest in divine joy, eager to meditate each day.

Misusing Divine Powers

Many meditators share a heartfelt concern: there was a time when their meditation reached profound heights, with divine experiences (*divya prakash, Anhad Naad*) flowing effortlessly, but now, even hours of practice feel empty, leaving them wondering what went wrong. I'll explain in a warm tone the subtle yet critical mistake behind this spiritual stagnation, why divine powers gained in meditation must never be misused, and how to regain that sacred connection. This will empower you to navigate deep meditative states with wisdom and balance, ensuring steady progress toward *Ishwar prapti.*

The Issue: From Divine Heights to Emptiness

Meditators often describe a golden phase where *Parampita Parmatma*'s grace opened spiritual treasures (*adhyatmik khazana*), granting divine visions (*divya prakash*), inner sounds (*Anhad Naad*), or even subtle powers (*roohani shaktiyan*). Yet, over time, despite dedicated practice, meditation feels hollow, as if they're "returning empty-handed" (*khaali haath*). This isn't a random loss but stems from a common, overlooked error that halts spiritual progress.

The Root Cause: Misusing Divine Powers

As meditation deepens, divine grace (*Ishwar aur guru kripa*) purifies the soul (*atma*), aligning it with its true essence. This brings extraordinary experiences and powers, such as:

- **Intuitive Insights**: Foreseeing future events (*bhavishya ghatna ka abhaas*) in waking life.
- **Supernatural Visions**: Seeing otherworldly phenomena (*aloukik cheezein*) with open eyes.
- **Other Abilities**: Subtle spiritual powers that transcend ordinary perception.

These are sacred gifts, but here's where the mistake happens:

- **The Temptation**: These powers feel thrilling (*romanchak*), tempting meditators to use them in worldly life (*sansarik jeevan*), either for personal gain or to alleviate suffering (e.g., resolving a crisis).
- **The Trap of Ego**: Using these powers rekindles ego (*ahankar*) and mental impurities (*man ki mail*), which took years to dissolve through meditation. The meditator begins feeling superior, disrupting inner peace.

- **The Divine Test**: These powers are a test from the divine (*Ishwariya pariksha*). Using them for worldly purposes (*sansarik swarth*) violates spiritual laws, halting progress. The divine withdraws these experiences until the meditator develops the capacity (*shamta*) to handle them responsibly.

Why Misuse Halts Progress

- **Spiritual Law**: Divine powers are granted only when a meditator's heart is pure and ego-free. Attempting to alter natural laws (*prakriti ke niyam*) or worldly circumstances through these powers signals attachment to *maya* (illusion), stalling advancement.
- **Loss of Grace**: Misuse disconnects you from divine grace, locking the "spiritual treasure" (*adhyatmik khazana*). No amount of meditation restores it until humility and surrender are regained.
- **Example from Life**: Like giving a child a sharp tool, divine powers are withheld if misused, as they could harm the meditator or others. Only when maturity (*shamta*) develops are they safely bestowed again.

Lessons from Saints

Great saints (*sant mahatma*), embodiments of *Parampita Parmatma*, exemplified this principle:

- **Humility Over Power**: Despite having disciples like kings and nawabs who offered palaces and wealth, saints like Guru Nanak or Kabir lived simply, earning their living through physical labor (*mehnat*). They shared their meager resources with others, never using spiritual powers (*roohani shakti*) for personal gain.
- **No Miracles for Show**: These saints could have performed miracles (*chamatkar*) or transcended death (*mrityu lok*), but they avoided such displays. Instead, they endured physical hardships to teach the true path (*satya ka marg*), guiding a few sincere souls across the ocean of existence (*bhavsagar*).
- **Respecting Karmic Law**: Saints upheld the laws of karma (*karm siddhant*), never altering worldly outcomes. If they, divine incarnations, respected these laws, an ordinary meditator (*saadhak*) has no capacity to bend them without consequences.

How to Avoid This Mistake

To prevent or recover from this spiritual setback, follow these steps:

1. **Preserve Sacred Gifts**:
    - Treat meditation-gained powers (*adhyatmik kamai*) as more precious than life itself. Never use them for worldly purposes (*sansarik swarth*), such as solving personal problems or impressing others.
    - Keep these experiences private, sharing only with a guru or trusted guide, as publicizing them fuels ego (*ahankar*).
2. **Stay Humble and Detached**:
    - When powers or visions arise, remain neutral (*sahaj*), neither chasing nor flaunting them. View them as divine grace, not personal achievements.
    - Avoid comparing yourself to others or feeling superior, as this rekindles ego, disrupting meditation.
3. **Balance Spiritual and Worldly Life**:
    - Live simply, fulfilling worldly duties (*sansarik jeevan*) with honesty, without relying on spiritual powers to ease challenges.
    - Accept life's joys and sorrows as karmic outcomes, surrendering to divine will, as saints did.
4. **Follow Guru's Teachings**:
    - Adhere strictly to your guru's guidance (*siksha*), focusing on *simran*, *Anhad Naad*, and selfless

> service (*seva*). These practices purify the mind, ensuring powers are used wisely.
> - Saints' lives show that true spirituality lies in humility and surrender, not in wielding powers.

For Those Who've Lost the Divine Connection

If you feel stuck, with meditation yielding no depth, you may have unknowingly misused divine powers. Here's how to reconnect:

- **Seek Forgiveness**: In daily meditation, sincerely ask *Parampita Parmatma* for forgiveness (*maafi*) with love (*prem*) and devotion (*bhakti*). Pray, "I erred; please restore your grace." The divine, an ocean of mercy (*prem aur maafi ka swaroop*), will forgive when your heart is pure.
- **Persistent Practice**: Continue *simran* and *Anhad Naad* daily, even if it feels empty. This rebuilds humility and purifies ego, reopening spiritual doors.
- **Surrender and Patience**: Trust that the divine will return the "key to the treasure" (*khazane ki chaabi*) when you're ready. Don't lose hope (*himmat na hare*), as divine love never abandons a sincere seeker.
- **Avoid Seeking External Help**: No one can intervene in this divine process.

For New Meditators Experiencing Powers

If you're beginning to sense supernatural phenomena (*aloukik anubhav*), take heed:

- **Learn from Others' Mistakes**: Don't repeat the error of misusing powers. Treat them as sacred (*jaan se zyada keemti*), guarding them fiercely.
- **No Worldly Use**: Even in dire circumstances (*sansaarik haalat*), resist using these powers. They're for spiritual growth, not worldly fixes.
- **Seek Guidance**: If confused, consult your guru or reflect in meditation, but avoid publicizing experiences, as it risks ego and distraction.

Maintaining balance (*santulan*) between spiritual (*adhyatmik*) and worldly life is crucial:

- Misusing powers disrupts this balance, tethering you to *maya* and halting progress.
- A single lapse (*galti*) can sever connection with divine energy (*divya shakti*), and regaining it may take years or lifetimes.
- Saints' lives teach that true liberation (*moksha*) comes from living simply, serving others, and surrendering to divine will, not chasing powers.

If your meditation feels empty, don't despair—it's a divine test to strengthen your humility and devotion. The mistake of misusing powers is common but reversible through sincere repentance and persistent *simran/Anhad Naad*. For new meditators, cherish your spiritual gifts, guarding them from worldly temptation. Follow saints' examples—live humbly, serve selflessly, and surrender to *Parampita Parmatma*. Your spiritual treasure awaits, locked only until your heart is ready. Meditate daily with love (*prem*), seek forgiveness, and trust divine mercy. Balance your worldly and spiritual lives, and never use divine powers for personal gain.

Why Some Meditators Feel Stuck

Many meditators feel disheartened when, despite years of practice, they experience no significant spiritual breakthroughs, while others using the same method report profound results. This frustration can lead to irregular practice or even abandoning meditation altogether. I'll explain in a warm, guiding tone why these challenges arise, how to choose the right meditation method based on your mind's state (*man ki avastha*), and why aligning your practice with your spiritual goal is key to success. This will empower you to find clarity, avoid discouragement, and progress steadily toward *Ishwar prapti*.

Meditators often compare their lack of experiences (e.g., *divya prakash*, *Anhad Naad*) to others' vivid accounts, leading to:

- **Frustration and Doubt**: Feeling "empty-handed" (*khaali haath*) despite effort breeds self-doubt, disrupting consistency.
- **Method-Hopping**: New meditators, overwhelmed by online options, switch methods frequently, fearing they're wasting time.

- **Core Issue**: The problem isn't the effort but a mismatch between the meditation method and the meditator's mental state (*man ki avastha*) or spiritual goal (*lakshya*). A method that's "nectar" (*amrit*) for one can cause confusion (*bhatkav*) for another if misaligned.

The Key: Matching Method to Mind's State

With hundreds of meditation methods, choosing the right one is the toughest step. Success is guaranteed if you select a method suited to your mind's state and practice with full devotion (*prem* and *shraddha*). To simplify this, let's categorize meditators based on their goals and mental states, helping you identify your path.

Seven Categories of Meditators

1. **Seeking Mental Peace**:
   - **Goal**: Achieve calm (*manasik shanti*) to balance family or worldly life, reduce anger (*gussa*), and make clear decisions.
   - **Mind's State**: Focused on stress relief, not spiritual awakening.
   - **Example**: Professionals or parents seeking emotional stability.

2. **Devotees of a Deity**:
     - **Goal**: Deepen love (*prem*) and devotion (*bhakti*) to their chosen deity (*ishta devta*, e.g., Krishna, God Shiva) through meditation alongside worship (*puja-path*).
     - **Mind's State**: Heart-driven, seeking divine connection.
     - **Example**: Those performing daily prayers and wanting meditative devotion.
3. **Kundalini Aspirants**:
     - **Goal**: Awaken Kundalini (*Maitreya shakti*), seen as divine energy, through specific practices.
     - **Mind's State**: Reverent toward divine feminine energy (*Adi Shakti*), often inspired by mystical traditions.
     - **Example**: Yogis drawn to chakra-based or energy-focused meditation.
4. **Self-Inquiry Seekers**:
     - **Goal**: Understand true self (*main kaun hoon*) or unravel life-death mysteries, prioritizing self-realization over divine experience (*Ishwarna anubhuti*).
     - **Mind's State**: Philosophical, less devotional, seeking existential truth.
     - **Example**: Those exploring Vedanta or Advaita.
5. **Yogic Practitioners**:

- ○ **Goal**: Awaken consciousness (*chetana shakti*) through physical yoga (*asanas*, *bandhas*, *pranayama*), aiming for cosmic knowledge (*Brahma gyan*).
  - ○ **Mind's State**: Focused on body and nervous system transformation.
  - ○ **Example**: Householders practicing yoga for spiritual growth.

6. **Tantric Aspirants**:
   - ○ **Goal**: Gain supernatural powers (*siddhis*) or energies through specialized meditation or mantras.
   - ○ **Mind's State**: Driven by curiosity about esoteric practices (*tantra yoga*).
   - ○ **Example**: Those seeking mystical or occult abilities.

7. **Seeking Truth**:
   - ○ **Goal**: Achieve complete liberation (*moksha*), escaping the cycle of birth and death (*janam-maran*), realizing worldly pleasures and pains are transient (*asthayi*).
   - ○ **Mind's State**: Detached, inspired by saints' wisdom (*sant gyan*), seeking ultimate truth.
   - ○ **Example**: Those meditating for spiritual freedom, like the speaker.

Choosing the Right Method

Each category requires a specific meditation method. Misalignment leads to stagnation, frustration, or even harm. Here's how to match:

1. **Mental Peace Seekers**:
    - **Suitable Method**: Guided meditation with music or breath awareness (*shwas dhyan*).
    - **Why**: These calm the mind without engaging deeper energies, ideal for stress relief.
    - **Avoid**: Mantra chanting (*jap*) or chakra meditation, as these awaken energies (*chetana shakti*) that disrupt mental and physical peace (*sharirik shanti*), causing distress.
    - **Example**: Listening to soothing music or focusing on breath for 10–20 minutes daily.
2. **Devotees**:
    - **Suitable Method**: Mantra chanting (*simran* or *jap*) of their deity's name (e.g., "Ram," "Waheguru").
    - **Why**: Keeps the mind anchored in devotion (*ishta bhakti*), progressing toward divine visions (*divya prakash*) or sounds (*Anhad Naad*).
    - **Avoid**: Witness meditation (*sakshi bhav*), where thoughts are observed neutrally. This detaches the mind

from the deity, creating a barrier (*bhatkav*) to devotion.

- o **Example**: After morning *puja*, chant a mantra with love for 30 minutes, focusing on the deity.

3. **Kundalini Aspirants**:
   - o **Suitable Method**: Kundalini meditation under a qualified guru's guidance, rooted in devotion (*shraddha*) to *Adi Shakti*.
   - o **Why**: Kundalini is a divine force (*daiviya shakti*), not a physical exercise. Without spiritual reverence, attempts lead to physical or mental issues (*sansarik samasya*).
   - o **Avoid**: Tutorials or articles, as they oversimplify Kundalini, risking harm without proper understanding.
   - o **Example**: Study Kundalini's spiritual aspects, then learn personally from a guru, practicing with faith.

4. **Self-Inquiry Seekers**:
   - o **Suitable Method**: Self-inquiry (*atma vichar*, e.g., "Who am I?") or witness meditation (*sakshi bhav*).
   - o **Why**: Aligns with their philosophical goal, fostering introspection without requiring divine devotion.

- o **Avoid**: *Anhad Naad* or mantra meditation, as lack of faith (*shraddha*) in divine sound or deities causes wandering (*bhatkav*) and frustration.
  - o **Example**: Reflect on "Who am I?" for 20 minutes daily, observing thoughts without attachment.

5. **Yogic Practitioners**:
   - o **Suitable Method**: Gentle yoga (*asanas*) or breathwork (*pranayama*) under guidance, avoiding extreme practices (*bandhas*).
   - o **Why**: Householders (*grihasthi*) can't sustain strict yogic disciplines (e.g., diet restrictions), and forced practices don't guarantee spiritual progress.
   - o **Avoid**: Complex *bandhas* or intense *pranayama* (e.g., *alom-vilom* with force), as these strain the nervous system without spiritual gain.
   - o **Example**: Practice simple *sukhasana* and slow breathing for 15 minutes, focusing on calm.

6. **Tantric Aspirants**:
   - o **Suitable Method**: None recommended here, as tantric practices (*tantra yoga*) require rare expertise and carry high risks.
   - o **Why**: Seeking powers (*siddhis*) often leads to ego (*ahankar*) and spiritual

stagnation. The speaker respectfully declines guidance, aligning with the seventh category.

- o **Avoid**: Self-taught tantra from online sources, as it's dangerous without a master.
- o **Example**: Redirect focus to simpler methods like *simran* or breath awareness.

7. **Truth Seekers**:
   - o **Suitable Method**: *Simran* and *Anhad Naad* meditation, rooted in faith in divine sound (*Brahma naad*).
   - o **Why**: Aligns with the goal of liberation (*moksha*), purifying the mind (*chitta shuddhi*) and transcending *maya* for divine union (*Ishwar prapti*).
   - o **Avoid**: Methods requiring physical strain (e.g., yoga *bandhas*) or lacking spiritual depth (e.g., music meditation), as they don't lead to liberation.
   - o **Example**: Chant a guru-given mantra for 30 minutes, then listen to *Anhad Naad* with devotion.

Why Experiences Differ

Even with the same method, experiences vary because:

- **Mind's State**: Each meditator's mental conditioning (*samskaras*), faith (*shraddha*), and goal differ, affecting outcomes.
- **Subtle Mistakes**: Small errors, like incorrect focus or lack of consistency, stall progress. For example, a devotee practicing *sakshi bhav* drifts from their deity, or a peace-seeker attempting chakra meditation faces unrest.
- **Karmic Timing**: Spiritual experiences (*anubhav*) unfold per divine will (*Parmatma ki kripa*) and past karma, not just effort.

Don't compare your journey to others'—their path reflects their mind's state, not yours. Instead, assess your method's alignment with your goal.

Overcoming Frustration and Confusion

To avoid discouragement and find the right path:

1. **Clarify Your Goal**:
    - Before each session, reflect: "Why am I meditating? What's my goal?" (*Dhyan kyun kar raha hoon? Lakshya kya hai?*)
    - If clear (e.g., *bhakti*, *moksha*), proceed confidently. If unclear,

revisit the seven categories to pinpoint your mind's state.
- A defined goal ensures no force (*Parma shakti*) can stop your progress, as divine grace (*Shivam*) opens paths.

2. **Stick to One Method**:
   - Choose a method matching your category and practice daily with love (*prem*) and faith (*shraddha*).
   - Consistency deepens focus (*ekagrata*), correcting small errors that block progress.
3. **Assess Mistakes**:
   - If progress stalls, evaluate your practice. Are you following the method correctly? Is it suited to your goal? For example, a peace-seeker using chakra meditation may need to switch to breath awareness.
4. **Avoid External Influences**:
   - Don't be swayed by hatha yoga (*asanas*, *bandhas*) or others' dramatic experiences. These distract householders and disrupt focus.
   - Trust your chosen method, as it's sacred to you (*pyari*).

5. **Patience and Devotion**:
   - Meditation opposes lifetimes of mental conditioning (*janmon ke samskaras*), requiring patience (*dhairya*) and love (*prem*).
   - Divine experiences come when the mind is ready, guided by *Parmatma*'s grace.

Special Note on Chakra Meditation

For those drawn to chakra awakening:

- **Prerequisite**: First resolve mental doubts (*shanka*) through spiritual knowledge (*adhyatmik gyan*). This "unties the mind's knots" (*man ki ganth*).
- **Natural Process**: With a purified mind, chakras open effortlessly (*sahaj*) during meditation, without physical effort (*sharirik prayas*).
- **Avoid Force**: Focusing on chakras prematurely, especially via online tutorials, risks physical and mental imbalance, as energy shifts overwhelm an unprepared body.

Feeling stuck or confused in meditation doesn't reflect a lack of devotion—it's often a small mismatch in method or goal. Identify your mind's state (*man ki avastha*) using the seven categories, choose a fitting method (e.g., *simran* for devotees, breath for peace-seekers), and practice daily with love (*prem*) and faith (*shraddha*). Before meditating, affirm your goal (*lakshya*). A clear heart unlocks divine grace (*Parma shakti*), guiding you to success. Whether seeking peace, devotion, or liberation, *Parmatma* paves your way.

Why Experiences Stop After Sharing

Many meditators share a poignant concern: during their practice, they had unique spiritual experiences (*anokha anubhav*), but after sharing them with others, those experiences vanished. This leads to fear that *Parmeshwar* (God) is punishing them, especially since they've heard that meditation experiences should remain private. Why sharing can disrupt progress, the spiritual principles behind this, and how to move forward without guilt or fear? This will empower you to navigate your meditation journey with clarity, humility, and renewed devotion, ensuring steady progress toward *Ishwar anubhuti* (divine realization).

Meditators often describe profound moments—like seeing intense light (*divya prakash*) or hearing *Anhad Naad*—that cease after being shared with others. This sparks worry that:

- They've angered *Parmeshwar*, who is withholding experiences as punishment (*saza*).
- A universal rule against sharing (*anubhav share na karna*) has been violated, causing spiritual loss.

The truth is gentler and rooted in the nature of the mind (*man*) and the spiritual path, not divine retribution.

The Spiritual Journey: A Quest for Self-Realization

Meditation (*dhyan sadhana*) is the soul's journey (*atma ka safar*) toward self-knowledge (*atmgyan*) and divine connection (*Ishwar anubhuti*). Saints and scriptures, like the *Upanishads*, *Vedanta*, and *Shri Guru Granth Sahib*, describe this as progressing through states:

- **Jagrut (Waking)** and **Swapna (Dream)** to **Sushupti (Deep Sleep)**, culminating in **Turiya** (Transcendental Consciousness), called the "Fourth State" (*Chautha Pad* or *Chauthi Pauri*).
- In *Turiya*, a meditator becomes a true *Gurmukh* (God-oriented), realizing their divine essence (*asli pehchaan*).

To reach this, the ego (*ahankar*, the sense of "I") must dissolve completely. Sharing experiences carelessly can disrupt this process, but not because of divine punishment.

Why Sharing Experiences Can Halt Progress

Saints advise against sharing meditation experiences, not as a strict rule but to protect the meditator's mind from ego (*ahankar*). The impact of sharing depends on *who* you share with and *why*. Let's explore with an example:

Scenario: Seeing Intense Light in Meditation

A meditator experiences bright light (*divya prakash*) during meditation, feels fear (*dar*), and is unsure how to proceed. They consider sharing this experience. Here's what happens with different people:

1. **Non-Meditating Friends**:
   - **Outcome**: Friends who don't meditate find the topic strange (*ajeeb*). They may dismiss it, ignore you, or label you "crazy" (*paagal*). Repeated attempts to explain frustrate you, draining your focus.
   - **Impact**: No spiritual harm, but the disconnect wastes energy and discourages you, as they can't guide you forward.
2. **Another Meditator Without Similar Experience**:
   - **Outcome**: You share with a fellow meditator who hasn't seen *divya prakash*. They can't advise you but may feel inferior, subtly altering their perception of you.

- o **Impact**:
  - ■ **On You**: Your mind registers you've surpassed another, planting seeds of ego (*ahankar*), like feeling "better" (*uttam*). This ego can grow, blocking deeper states.
  - ■ **On Them**: They may view you as superior, asking questions about *divya prakash*, which reinforces your ego. Their subtle flattery (*baaton mein uttam batana*) feeds pride, distancing you from humility.
- o **Why It Halts**: Ego is the opposite of the egoless state (*ahankar mukt*) needed for *Turiya*. Experiences fade as the mind shifts from divine focus to self-importance.

3. **A Knowledgeable, Detached Guide**:
   - o **Outcome**: You find someone experienced (*yogya vyakti*), perhaps a stranger, who understands your state. They offer clear guidance without personal attachment, pointing you to the next step.
   - o **Impact**:
     - ■ **On You**: You feel respect (*adar*) for their wisdom, but no ego arises, as the

interaction is purely spiritual, not personal.

- **On Them**: If they're realized (*Parampad prapt*), they remain unaffected by praise or titles (*guru, sant*), knowing all knowledge comes from *Parmeshwar*. They see no difference between you and themselves, maintaining humility.
  - **Why It Helps**: Sharing with such a guide advances your journey without ego, as the focus stays on divine truth (*satya*).

The Key Question: What's Your Intention?

The problem isn't sharing itself but the mind's intention (*ichchha*) behind it. Ask yourself:

- **Am I sharing to impress or influence others?** If so, this is the mind's trick (*man ka chaal*) that saints warn against. Seeking validation (*prabhavit karna*) fuels ego, disrupting meditation's egoless goal. Experiences stop as *Parmeshwar*'s grace pauses to protect you from pride.
- **Am I sharing to resolve a doubt or seek guidance?** If you're genuinely seeking help (*jigyasa ka haal*), sharing with a qualified

guide (e.g., guru, realized soul) is beneficial and aligns with the path.

Saints don't forbid asking questions (*sawal poochhna*) about experiences—they encourage seeking clarity from those who can guide without personal bias. Every realized soul (*atmgyani*) has been guided by another, showing sharing for growth is valid.

Is God Punishing You?

Absolutely not. *Parmeshwar* doesn't punish for sharing experiences. The cessation of experiences is a natural consequence of ego (*ahankar*) arising, not divine wrath. *Parmeshwar* is pure love (*prem*) and mercy (*daya*), always ready to forgive and guide. The pause in experiences is a gentle nudge to realign with humility and devotion (*shraddha*).

How to Move Forward

If you've shared experiences carelessly and feel stuck, here's how to restore your practice:

1. **Seek Forgiveness**:
    - In your next meditation, sit in your posture (*dhyan asan*) and sincerely pray to *Parmeshwar*. "I made a mistake (*galti*) by sharing to impress.

Please forgive me (*maafi*). Guide me back to your grace."

- Offer this prayer with love (*prem*) and faith (*shraddha*), trusting *Parmeshwar*'s mercy.

2. **Resolve to Be Mindful**:
   - Take a vow (*sankalp*): "I'll only share experiences to resolve doubts (*jigyasa*) with a qualified guide, not to impress others."
   - This commitment protects your mind from ego's traps.

3. **Resume Meditation with Confidence**:
   - Let go of the fear (*shanka*) that *Parmeshwar* will punish you. Start meditating daily with full devotion, asking only for divine connection.
   - Consistency rebuilds humility, reopening spiritual experiences.

4. **Guard Future Experiences**:
   - Treat new experiences as sacred (*pavitra*), sharing only with a guru or realized guide who understands your state.
   - Avoid casual discussions, even with fellow meditators, to prevent ego (*ahankar*) from creeping in.

The Bigger Picture

The first step in spiritual awakening (*spiritual awakening*) is mental clarity (*vaicharik jagruti*). Recognize when your mind seeks validation versus genuine growth. Meditation is about dissolving the "I" to merge with *Parmeshwar*. Sharing experiences with the wrong intention strengthens the "I," stalling progress. By sharing wisely—with a guide, for clarity—you align with saints' teachings and advance toward *Turiya*.

If you've lost experiences after sharing, don't fear divine punishment—*Parmeshwar* loves you and awaits your return. The pause reflects ego (*ahankar*), not anger. Today, pray for forgiveness (*maafi*) with love (*prem*), vow to share only for guidance, and resume meditation without doubt (*nisch nisch*). For all meditators, guard experiences like treasures, sharing only with a guru or selfless guide (*yogya vyakti*) to resolve doubts, not to impress. Your soul's journey (*atma ka safar*) to *Ishwar anubhuti* is sacred. Every step, even mistakes, teaches humility. Meditate daily with *prem* and *shraddha*, trusting *Parmeshwar* to reopen divine doors. If my words hurt anyone, I seek forgiveness.

Are Long Hours of Chanting Necessary?

Some meditators worry after seeing people claiming that chanting mantras (*simran*) for 12+ hours is necessary to reach deep meditative states (*shunya avastha* or *sushupti*), making their 15–60 minutes of daily practice feel inadequate. This doubt (*shanka*) can discourage them, questioning how they'll ever progress. I'll share a practical guide to a powerful technique that helps achieve deep meditation in minutes, debunk the myth of marathon chanting, and empower you to focus with confidence and joy, ensuring steady progress toward *Ishwar prapti*

Meditators often encounter people showcasing extended mantra chanting (10–18 hours), suggesting it's the only path to profound states like *shunya* (void) or *sushupti* (deep stillness). This creates:

- **Doubt (*Shanka*)**: Those practicing 15–60 minutes daily fear their efforts are insufficient, undermining confidence.
- **Discouragement**: Comparing themselves to supposed "12-hour chanters," they feel their *bhakti* or *sadhana* is lacking.
- **Confusion**: They wonder if short sessions can ever lead to deep meditation.

The Core Principle of Meditation

To understand the technique, grasp meditation's essence:

- **Two Constant Processes**:
    - **Breathing (*Shwas*)**: Runs automatically, requiring no effort to take the next breath.
    - **Thoughts (*Vichar*)**: The mind (*man*) never stops thinking, even when you try to be thought-free, continuing in dreams (*sapna*).
- **Meditation's Goal**: Detach from the body, mind, and intellect (*buddhi*) to access divine knowledge (*param gyan*). This requires:
    - Slowing breath (*shwas ki gati*), which calms thoughts (*vicharon ki gati*).
    - Focusing the mind on a single point, like a mantra, to still it (*shithil*).
- **The Challenge**: During mantra chanting, the mind wanders unnoticed, despite hours of effort. As Kabir Ji said, "The rosary turns in hand, the tongue chants, but the mind roams in ten directions—this isn't true simran" (*Mala to kar mein phire, jeebh phire mukh maahi, manuva to dasha disha phire, yeh to sumiran naahi*).
- **Encouragement**: Every meditator faces this wandering mind—it's a universal stage, not a failure.

The Technique: Reverse Counting for Deep Focus

This method, refined through the speaker's own struggles, builds mental focus (*ekagrata*) in minutes, leading to deep meditative states (*shunya* or *sushupti*). It works for both mantra (*simran*) and breath (*shwas dhyan*) practitioners.

For Mantra Practitioners (*Simran*)

1. **Prepare**:
    - Sit in your meditation posture (*dhyan asan*), comfortable and relaxed.
    - Pray to *Parmpita Parmeshwar* for guidance and focus.
2. **Reverse Counting (Five Rounds)**:
    - Mentally count backward from 100 to 0 (*man hi man*), e.g., "100, 99, 98…" until zero.
    - Repeat this cycle five times, restarting at 100 after reaching zero.
    - Focus solely on the numbers, noting when your mind wanders (e.g., forgetting a number or skipping).
3. **Chant Mantra**:
    - After five rounds (taking ~5–10 minutes), begin mantra chanting (*simran*) for at least 20 minutes.
    - If the mind drifts, briefly recall Kabir's words to gently scold yourself: "Why

is my mind wandering instead of focusing on *Parmeshwar*?"
  - Optionally, count mantra repetitions mentally (e.g., "mantra 1, mantra 2…"), noting when you lose track, to highlight distractions.

4. **Observe Progress**:
  - Initially, you'll notice frequent wandering (e.g., missing numbers or mantra counts), revealing your mind's restlessness (*ashanti*).
  - Within days, the mind stabilizes, missing fewer counts, as it learns to stay present (*andar thaharna*).

For Breath Practitioners (*Shwas Dhyan*)

- Follow the same steps, but count backward mentally while observing your breath:
  - Inhale: "100," exhale: "99," inhale: "98," exhale: "97," etc.
  - Complete five rounds, then focus on breath alone for 10–20 minutes without counting.
  - If distracted, resume counting briefly to refocus.

Variations

- **Language**: Count in any comfortable language (e.g., Hindi, English, or your native tongue).
- **Pace**: Count steadily, not rushed, to maintain awareness.

Why This Works

- **Reverse Counting** trains the mind to focus (*ekagrata*):
    - Counting backward is unfamiliar, requiring effort, exposing the mind's restlessness (e.g., forgetting numbers).
    - Repeating five rounds builds mental discipline, teaching the mind to "pause" (*thaharana*), countering its wandering nature.
- **Immediate Feedback**: Missing a number signals distraction, helping you catch and correct wandering instantly, unlike mantra chanting where hours pass unnoticed.
- **Stills the Mind**: Focused counting slows breath and thoughts, preparing the mind for deep mantra or breath meditation.
- **Universal Application**: Works for both *simran* (anchoring mantra) and *shwas dhyan* (calming breath), aligning with saints' insights that a still mind (*shithil man*) unlocks spiritual progress.

The Results

- **Short-Term (Days–Weeks)**:
    - Within days, you'll notice fewer missed counts, with your mind staying present longer.
    - After 20 minutes of focused *simran*, you'll feel *shanti* (peace) and glimpses of stillness (*shunya*).
    - The mind merges with the mantra's rhythm (*lay*), feeling like a single chant (*ek mantra*).
- **Deeper States (Weeks–Years)**:
    - In minutes, you'll you'll enter *sushupti* (or *shunya* (, losing awareness of body, mind, and mantra (*hoosh na rahna*).
    - Initially, this feels like falling asleep, but soon, you'll distinguish it as meditative depth (*gahra dhyan*).
    - Over time, sessions extend (*minutes to hours*), with states like *ardha samadhi* (partial absorption) and *poorna samadhi* (full absorption).
    - Returning, you'll feel infinite peace (*aseem shanti*) and joy (*anand*), indescribable in words (*shabdon mein bayan nahi*).
    - Physical sensations (*chetana*) return slowly, with the body feeling "stone-like" (*jad*), and brief

disorientation (*e.g., forgetting time or place*).

Why Short, Focused Practice Suffices

- **Quality Over Quantity**: 20 minutes of fully focused *simran* (no missed mantra counts) surpasses hours of distracted chanting. The reverse counting method ensures this focus.
- **Saints' Wisdom**: Saints like Kabir emphasize mental stillness (*man ki shithilta*), not marathon efforts. A concentrated mind enters *shunya* quickly.
- **Divine Grace (*Kripa*)**: *Parmpita Parmeshwar* rewards devotion (*prem*) and focus, not mere hours.

Don't let 12-hour chanting claims shake your faith—your 15–60 minutes of *simran* or *shwas dhyan* is enough if done with focus (*ekagrata*). The reverse counting method (100 to 0, five times) trains your mind to stay present, leading to deep meditation (*shunya, sushupti*) in minutes. Forget marathon myths; those videos loop short recordings, not reflecting true *sadhana*.

Start today: before *simran*, count backward five times, then chant with love (*prem*) and faith (*shraddha*). For breath meditators, count with breaths. You'll feel your mind centering daily, merging with *Parmeshwar*'s grace. Kabir's words guide us: a wandering mind isn't *simran*, but persistence wins. Your journey to *param gyan* shines through focused moments, not endless hours.

Visions of Divine Forms

Many meditators share that during meditation, they see divine forms like Lord Shiva, Krishna, Mataji, Kabir Ji, or Guru Nanak Ji, based on their devotion (*bhakti*) and faith (*shraddha*). They ask which meditative state this is and what to do next. This stage is pivotal: it can lead to wandering (*bhatkav*) or, with patience (*dhairya*), to the profound state of divine light (*divya prakash*). What this stage means, how to avoid pitfalls, and how to progress to *divya prakash*?

When meditators see their chosen deity (*ishta devta*) or guru during meditation, it's a significant yet delicate stage:

- **What It Is**: This is a transitional state where the subconscious mind (*avchetan man*) projects divine images, driven by your devotion (*prem* and *bhakti*).
- **Potential Risks**: Misinterpreting these visions can lead to spiritual wandering (*bhatkav*), stalling progress.
- **Potential Reward**: With proper practice, this stage can lead to *divya prakash*, a

milestone in spiritual awakening (*adhyatmik yatra*).

Why These Visions Occur

To understand this stage, consider the mind's behavior:

- **Daily Life**: Your body and mind are active, engaged in tasks (*dincharya*).
- **Meditation**: Sitting in meditation (*dhyan*), physical activity stops, but the mind isn't instantly calm (*shant*). Techniques like breath focus (*shwas dhyan*) or mantra chanting (*simran*) are used to quiet it.
- **Mind's Shift**: As the body becomes still (*jad*), the mind slows (*shithil*), and brain activity diminishes. The subconscious activates, similar to dreaming during sleep, where the body is inactive, but the subconscious creates visions.
- **Divine Images**: In meditation, the subconscious projects the divine form (*swaroop*) you revere—Shiva, Krishna, or Guru Nanak—based on your devotion or the images (*murti*, *photo*) you worship. These are reflections of your inner *bhakti*, not necessarily the deity's true form (*asli roop*).

The Pitfall: Misinterpreting Visions

This stage can mislead if not handled wisely:

- **Mistake 1: Assuming True Divinity**: If the vision matches your worshipped image (*murti* or *photo*), you might believe it's *Parmeshwar*'s actual form (*Ishwar anubhuti*). This is premature, as it's a subconscious projection (*avchetan man ki kriya*), not the ultimate divine essence.
- **Mistake 2: Engaging with Visions**: Some meditators try to converse with the form, asking questions or seeking solutions to worldly problems (*sansarik samasya*). This ties the mind to *maya* (illusion), pulling you away from spiritual progress.
- **Consequence**: Craving daily visions (*har roz darshan*) traps you in this stage, preventing deeper states. Doubts (*shanka*) arise about your practice, guru, or deity, causing spiritual and worldly confusion (*bhatkav*).
- **Mental Imagery vs. Devotion**: If you actively imagine the form (*dimagi kalpana*), it's a fleeting mental creation (*man ki rachna*), not sustainable. True visions arise spontaneously from *bhakti*, not forced visualization.

How to Progress to *Divya Prakash*

To move beyond this stage and reach *divya prakash*, follow these steps with patience (*dhairya*) and focus (*ekagrata*):

1. **Stay Calm and Neutral**:
   - When a divine form (*ishta* or *guru swaroop*) appears in the darkness behind closed eyes (*andhkar*), avoid excitement (*utsahit*) or disturbance (*vichlit*). Don't analyze or seek meaning.
   - Recognize it as a subconscious projection, not the ultimate *Ishwar*.
2. **Focus on the Face**:
   - Gently center your attention on the face of the form, not the entire body. Avoid examining details (*parakhna*) or wandering across the image.
   - Gaze with love (*prem*) and faith (*shraddha*), as if beholding your deity or guru with reverence.
3. **Practice Inner *Tratak***:
   - This stage is called *guru dhyan* or inner *tratak dhyan* (focused gazing). Hold your focus on the face as long as it remains, without forcing it to stay.
   - If the form fades, don't search for it or imagine it again. This keeps the mind free from attachment.
4. **Return to Your Method**:
   - When the vision disappears, resume your meditation technique:
     - If chanting (*simran*), restart your mantra.

- If breath-focused (*shwas dhyan*), return to observing breaths.
  - Avoid dwelling on the vision to maintain focus.

5. **Observe the Transformation**:
   - With consistent practice, the form's duration increases. As you focus on the face, it gradually dissolves into light (*prakash roop*).
   - If you sustain focus during this shift, a brilliant light (*divya prakash*) emerges, brighter than anything seen with open eyes.

6. **Handle the Light with Calm**:
   - The sudden *divya prakash* may startle you, causing eyes to open. You might see light even with open eyes, creating awe or fear.
   - Don't panic—this is normal. Within seconds or minutes, vision normalizes , and you feel stable.
   - This is a distinct method (*vidhi*) of *divya prakash darshan* via *guru* or *ishta swaroop*.

For Those Without Visions

If you don't see divine forms, don't feel discouraged:

- **Other Paths to *Divya Prakash***: Mantra chanting (*simran*), breath meditation (*shwas dhyan*), or *Anhad Naad* also lead to *divya prakash*. For *Anhad Naad* practitioners, merging with subtle sounds (*sukshma dhun*) brings both sound and light experiences.
- **Universal Milestone**: *Divya Prakash* is a key stage (*padav*) in all meditation methods, marking the start of true spiritual progress (*asli adhyatmik yatra*).
- **Trust Your Practice**: Physical or mental sensations before *divya prakash* are minor milestones (*chhote parv*). Focus on your method, trusting it will lead to light or sound.

Why *Divya Prakash* and *Anhad Naad* Matter

- **Two Forms of One Power**: *Divya Prakash* (divine light) and *Anhad Naad* (divine sound) are dual expressions of the same divine energy (*shakti*). They're reliable markers of spiritual depth, unlike visions, which can be subconscious projections.
- **Beyond Visions**: Don't cling to divine forms or other phenomena (*shakti, darshan*). Only *divya prakash* and *Anhad Naad* guide you to true awakening, as they transcend mental imagery (*man ki rachna*).

Avoiding Spiritual Wandering (*Bhatkav*)

To prevent getting stuck:

- **Don't Chase Visions**: Seeking daily darshan (*har roz darshan*) traps you in the subconscious stage, blocking *divya prakash*.
- **Avoid Worldly Questions**: Don't ask the form about worldly issues (*sansarik samasya*). This pulls you into *maya*, not divinity.
- **Stay Detached**: View visions as stepping stones, not the goal. Let them arise and fade naturally, returning to *simran* or *shwas dhyan*.
- **Trust Your *Bhakti***: The vision reflects your love (*prem*) for your *ishta* or *guru*, but it's a projection, not the ultimate truth (*satya*).

Seeing your *ishta devta* or *guru* in meditation is a beautiful sign of your *bhakti*, but it's a delicate stage. Don't mistake it for *Ishwar anubhuti*—it's your subconscious (*avchetan man*) reflecting your devotion. To progress, focus on the form's face with *prem* and *shraddha*, practicing inner *tratak* until it transforms into *divya prakash*. If the vision fades, return to *simran* or *shwas dhyan* without chasing it. If you don't see forms, trust your method—*Anhad Naad* or mantra will also lead to *divya prakash*. This stage isn't the end but the start of your true spiritual journey (*adhyatmik yatra*). Avoid wandering by staying detached from visions and worldly desires. Every sensation is a milestone, but only *divya prakash* and *Anhad Naad* anchor your path to *Parmeshwar*. Meditate daily with patience (*dhairya*), and divine grace (*kripa*) will guide you.

Sleepiness in Meditation

Many meditators express frustration about falling asleep during meditation, a common issue that disrupts their practice and focus, especially at the third eye (*ajna chakra*). While sleepiness isn't harmful initially, overcoming it is essential to deepen your meditation and extend session time, particularly for those struggling to focus on the third eye. I'll share an experience-based guide to prevent sleepiness, enhance focus, and naturally increase meditation duration, empowering you to progress confidently toward deeper spiritual states (*Ishwar prapti*).

Meditators often find themselves dozing off within minutes of starting meditation, despite enthusiasm (*utsah*). This leads to:

- **Frustration**: Inability to maintain awareness or focus, especially on the third eye (*ajna chakra*).
- **Short Sessions**: Sleep cuts practice time, hindering progress to advanced states (*agla avastha*).

- **Wandering Mind**: Difficulty sustaining mantra chanting (*simran*) or listening to divine sounds (*Anhad Naad*), as thoughts drift.

Why Sleepiness Occurs

Sleepiness during meditation arises from two key mental processes:

1. **Seeing Power** (*Dekhne ki Shakti*): When you close your eyes, you see darkness (*andhkar*). If the mind wanders, it projects mental images (e.g., faces, scenes from the office or home), pulling focus outward.
2. **Thinking Power** (*Sochne ki Shakti*): The mind constantly generates thoughts (*vichar*), even when you try to stop them. These thoughts create mental "pictures" (*tasveerein*), leading to distraction and eventually sleep.

When the mind shifts from meditation (e.g., *simran* or *Anhad Naad*) to external thoughts or images, you lose awareness and drift into sleep (*neend*), often without realizing it.

The Solution: Channeling Seeing and Thinking Powers

To prevent sleep and deepen meditation, you must redirect these two powers inward, maintaining awareness and focus. Here's a step-by-step method:

1. Anchor the Seeing Power in Darkness (*Andhkar*)

- **How**:
    - Close your eyes gently (*sahaj*) during meditation, observing the natural darkness behind them (*andhkar*).
    - Avoid straining eyes or searching for images. Let darkness remain without effort—no pressure (*dabav*) on eyes.
    - As long as you're aware of this darkness, your focus is inward, and sleep cannot overtake you.
- **What to Watch For**:
    - If faces, places, or scenes (e.g., office, home) appear, your mind has wandered. These are mental projections, not spiritual experiences.
    - Immediately return to your meditation technique:
        - **Mantra (*Simran*)**: Resume chanting.
        - **Anhad Naad**: Listen to the divine sound.
        - **Breath (*Shwas Dhyan*)**: Focus on breathing.

- **Why It Works**:
    - Staying with darkness keeps the seeing power inward, preventing mental imagery that leads to sleep.
    - Avoiding eye strain ensures a relaxed, sustainable focus, aiding third-eye concentration (*ajna chakra*).

2. Anchor the Thinking Power in Mantra (*Simran*)

- **How**:
    - Continuously chant your mantra (*jap*) or listen to *Anhad Naad*, ensuring the mind repeats only the mantra or sound (*shabd*).
    - If thoughts shift to external topics (e.g., people, objects, daily tasks), recognize this instantly (*jagrukta*) and redirect the mind to *simran* or *Naad*.
    - Be vigilant: the mind's habit is to think relentlessly (*din-raat vichar*), creating a "storm of thoughts" (*vicharon ki aandhi*). Mantra chanting reins it in.
- **What to Watch For**:
    - When thoughts stray (e.g., planning, memories), the mind pulls the seeing

power outward, projecting images. This sequence—thoughts to images—leads to sleep.
  - Act quickly to refocus on *simran* before images form, maintaining mental clarity.
- **Why It Works**:
  - A mantra occupies the thinking power, reducing random thoughts.
  - Consistent redirection strengthens mental discipline, stabilizing focus on the third eye.

3. Daily Practice for Mastery

- **Routine**:
  - Sit in a comfortable posture (*asan*), keeping the spine straight (*reedh sidhi*).
  - Begin with *simran*, *Anhad Naad*, or *shwas dhyan*, applying the above steps.
  - Each time the mind wanders (images or thoughts), gently return to darkness and mantra without frustration.
- **Progress**:
  - Within days, the mind stops projecting external images, as it learns to stay inward.

- Random thoughts decrease, extending meditation time naturally (*automatic*).
- Focus on the third eye (*ajna chakra*) strengthens, as distractions no longer pull you away.

Additional Benefits

- **Extended Sessions**: With fewer thoughts and no sleep, you'll meditate longer effortlessly, as the mind stays engaged.
- **Third-Eye Focus**: Reduced mental chatter (*vicharon ka tootna*) stabilizes attention at the *ajna chakra*, paving the way for advanced states (*divya prakash, Anhad Naad*).
- **Physical Stability**: Fewer distractions minimize physical shifts (e.g., body adjustments), enhancing meditative depth.

Common Tips (But Not Enough Alone)

- **Limitation**: Even with these, sleepiness persists for many, as they don't address the root cause—uncontrolled seeing and thinking powers.
- **Focus on Basics**: The proposed method tackles the mind's core tendencies, offering a direct solution.

Reassurance: A Proven Method

- **Guarantee**: With daily practice (*roz ka abhyas*), you'll overcome sleep within days, noticing sharper focus and extended meditation time.
- **Third-Eye Progress**: Those struggling with *ajna chakra* focus will find their attention naturally settling there, unlocking deeper states.

Addressing Doubts

- **Not a Spiritual Experience**: Images seen during distraction (e.g., faces, scenes) are mental illusions (*man ke chhalave*), not divine visions (*satya anubhav*). True experiences occur when body and eye awareness fades (*sharir ka khyal nahi*).

Falling asleep in meditation is a common hurdle, not a failure. By channeling your seeing power (*andhkar* focus) and thinking power (*simran* focus), you'll overcome sleep in days, extend your sessions, and stabilize third-eye focus (*ajna chakra*). Don't chase images or thoughts—they're mental traps (*chhalave*), not divine truths. Return to *simran*, *Anhad Naad*, or *shwas dhyan* with alertness (*jagrukta*), and watch your practice deepen.

Who am I?

Many meditators grapple with the profound question "Who am I?" (*Main kaun hoon?*) and struggle with a restless mind that wanders during meditation, overwhelmed by a storm of thoughts. Some chant "Who am I?" like a mantra, similar to others chanting traditional mantras or divine names (*nam jap*), while others feel frustrated that their mind won't settle (*man dhyan mein nahi lagta*). I'll dive into an insightful exploration of the mind's nature, using the analogy of a day in the life of "Ram" to unravel the "Who am I?" inquiry. This will empower you to tame your mind's chatter, deepen your meditation, and move closer to self-realization (*atmgyan*) and divine connection (*Ishwar prapti*).

The Core Issues

Meditators face two intertwined challenges:

1. **The Question "Who am I?"**: This universal inquiry drives spiritual seekers, whether they chant it as a mantra or ponder it philosophically. Understanding its depth is crucial, even for those chanting other mantras (*simran, guru shabd*).
2. **Restless Mind in Meditation**: The mind's constant activity—producing random thoughts, scenes (*drishya*), and doubts (*shanka*)—prevents focus, making

meditation feel like a battle. Meditators wonder: *What is this mind, and how do I control it?*

Understanding the Mind: The Story of Ram

Ram's Day: A Cycle of Body and Mind

- **Morning**: Ram wakes, and his mind immediately churns: *What's today's plan? What's pending from yesterday?* . These thoughts drive his routine—morning rituals (*nitya karma*), breakfast, and heading to work.
- **Daytime**: As Ram leaves home, his mind bombards him with work, problems, and plans. His intellect (*vivek*) organizes tasks, but the mind keeps him entangled in thoughts, even during breaks or lunch. Ram identifies fully with his body and name, never questioning his essence.
- **Evening**: Ram returns home, eats, and sleeps, his mind still active with thoughts. At no point does he wonder, *Am I more than this body? Who am I?* The mind and intellect accept the body (*sharir roopi Ram*) as his sole identity (*astitva*).

- **Key Observation**: The mind convinces Ram he is his body, name, and roles, leaving no room for deeper inquiry.

Ram's Sleep: Dreams and Deep Sleep

- **Dream State**: Ram dreams, seeing himself acting, talking, or moving, identical to the daytime Ram. Yet, his physical body lies asleep. This raises a question: *If Ram's body is asleep, who is seeing the dream? Who is the dream-Ram acting and thinking?*
  - **Subconscious Explanation**: Dreams arise from the subconscious mind (*avchetan man*), reflecting daytime thoughts (*chintan*). But *Who is the experiencer beyond the body and dream?*
- **Deep Sleep**: Occasionally, Ram experiences dreamless sleep, recalling only lying down and waking up, with 6–8 hours unaccounted for (*kahan tha?*). No body, no dream-Ram, no thoughts exist. *Where was Ram during this void? Who was absent?*
- **Key Question**: Across waking, dreaming, and deep sleep, *who is the real Ram?* If the body-Ram sleeps, the dream-Ram vanishes, and no Ram exists in deep sleep, *who are we truly?*

Connecting to Meditation

These three states—waking (*jagrit*), dreaming (*swapna*), and deep sleep (*sushupti*)—mirror meditative experiences:

- **Initial Meditation**: Like Ram's waking state, the mind wanders, distracted by thoughts or scenes (*drishya*). You chant mantras (*simran*) or focus, but identify with the body (*main hi dhyan kar raha hoon*), assuming it's experiencing meditation.
- **Deeper Meditation**: As focus deepens, visions or dream-like scenes appear, akin to the dream state. If you doze off, dreams may intrude. The mind links these to the body (*sharir ne anubhav kiya*), reinforcing the "I am the body" illusion.
- **Profound Meditation**: In rare moments, you lose awareness of mantra, body, and thoughts (*mantra bhool jata hai*), entering a void-like state for seconds or minutes. No body, mind, or world exists, yet an infinite bliss (*aseem anand*) arises upon returning. *Who experiences this bliss if the body and mind are absent?*

The Mind's Game: A Barrier to Truth

The mind (*man*) is the obstacle to answering "Who am I?":

- **Illusion of Identity**: It convinces you that you are the body, name (e.g., Ram), and thoughts, never questioning this identity during daily life or shallow meditation.

- **Restlessness in Meditation**: The mind generates endless thoughts, doubts (*shanka* about *sadhana* or guru's teachings), and clever arguments (*daleel*), claiming intelligence (*chaturai*). It resists focus, pulling you into distractions.
- **Ego's Role**: The mind clings to ego (*ahankar*), proud of its thoughts, knowledge, or existence. This ego blocks deep meditation, as it fears losing control when faced with the unknown.
- **Intellect's Limitation**: Your intellect (*vivek*) recognizes meditation's supremacy, but the mind overrides it with doubts and distractions.

The Solution: One Question to Tame the Mind

To counter the mind's restlessness and deepen meditation, ask it a single question whenever it wanders:

- **The Question**: *If I am this body, who sees the dream when the body sleeps? If no body or mind exists in deep sleep, who experiences the bliss in deep meditation? (Agar main yeh sharir hoon, toh swapna kaun dekhta hai? Sushupti mein koi nahi,*

toh dhyan ka anand kaun mehsoos karta hai?)
- **How to Use It**:
    - Before meditating, reflect briefly (a few moments) on Ram's story: the waking body, dream-Ram, and absence in deep sleep. Realize the body, mind, and intellect aren't the true "you" (*asli Ram*).
    - During meditation, when the mind wanders (e.g., thoughts, scenes, doubts), pause and ask: *Who am I, if not this body or mind?* Since the mind has no answer (*jawab nahi*), it quiets, allowing focus to return to *simran* or breath (*shwas dhyan*).
- **Why It Works**:
    - The question exposes the mind's illusion (*man ka chhal*), forcing it to confront its ignorance.
    - It shifts attention from distractions to the inquiry (*main kaun hoon?*), aligning with the goal of self-realization (*atmgyan*).
    - Repeated use weakens the mind's ego (*ahankar*), fostering surrender (*samarpan*) and focus (*ekagrata*).

Deepening the "Who am I?" Inquiry

For those chanting "Who am I?" or other mantras (*simran, guru shabd*):

- **Not Just a Chant**: Treat "Who am I?" as a profound inquiry, not a mechanical repetition. Reflect on Ram's states to understand the self beyond body and mind.
- **For All Meditators**: Whether chanting "Ram," "Soham," or focusing on *Anhad Naad*, the inquiry applies. The mind's restlessness is universal, and questioning its identity (*man kaun hai?*) centers it.
- **Beyond the Body**: Recognize that meditative bliss (*aseem anand*) isn't the body's, mind's, or intellect's—it belongs to the true self (*asli Ram*), a divine power (*shakti*) within.

Overcoming the Mind's Resistance

The mind resists deep meditation because:

- **Ego's Fear**: It clings to its identity (*ahankar*), recoiling when challenged. Admitting "I know nothing" (*main kuch nahi janta*) threatens its pride.
- **Wall of Thoughts**: Doubts, confusion, and mental weaving form a barrier between you and self-knowledge (*atmgyan*).
- **Solution**: Embrace surrender (*samarpan*) with love (*prem*) and faith (*shraddha*). Accept the mind's ignorance, letting go of its cleverness (*chaturai*).

Practical Steps for Meditation

1. **Pre-Meditation Reflection**:
   - Before starting, spend a moment contemplating: *This body, mind, and intellect are not me. The true me experiences bliss beyond them.* Recall Ram's waking, dreaming, and deep sleep states.
   - Affirm: *I meditate to know the real me, not to satisfy this body or mind.*
2. **During Meditation**:
   - Begin with your practice (*simran, shwas dhyan,* or "Who am I?" inquiry).
   - When the mind wanders (thoughts, scenes, doubts), ask: *Who am I? Who experiences this?* Since it can't answer, it calms, refocusing on your practice.
   - If chanting "Who am I?", pair it with reflection: *Am I this body, mind, or the witness of bliss?*
3. **Persist with Surrender**:
   - Daily meditation weakens the mind's grip. Where the mind yields and surrenders ego, your spiritual journey begins.
   - Trust that the true self (*asli Ram*) and divine power (*Parmpita Parmatma*) guide you.

The Bigger Picture

- **Meditation's Purpose**: It's a battle to transcend the body, mind, and intellect (*shatir dimag*), revealing the true self (*asli swaroop*). Mantra chanting (*jap*) and meditation dismantle the ego's wall.
- **True Self as Divine**: The bliss in deep meditation (*aseem anand*) belongs to the divine spark within (*Ram roop shakti*), not the body or mind. This spark seeks union with *Parmatma* (*Ishwar darshan*).
- **Mind as Ally**: By humbling the mind (*main kuch nahi janta*), it becomes a tool for liberation, not an obstacle.

Your mind's restlessness and endless thoughts aren't your enemy—they're a call to explore "Who am I?" Through Ram's story, see that you're not the body, mind, or intellect, but the divine essence (*shakti*) experiencing bliss beyond (*aseem anand*). In meditation, when thoughts arise, ask: *Who am I, if not this body or mind?* This question silences the mind's chatter, deepening your practice (*simran* or inquiry).

The mind's ego (*ahankar*) resists, but surrender (*samarpan*) with love (*prem*) and faith (*shraddha*) unlocks profound states. Reflect daily before meditating: the body and mind are temporary; the true you (*asli Ram*) is eternal (*shashvat*). This vast truth unfolds with repeated contemplation .

Stagnation at Initial Sounds

Many meditators practicing *Anhad Naad* (divine sound) meditation report hearing only initial sounds like silence (*sannata*), crickets (*jheengur*), or small birds chirping (*chhoti chidiyon ke chahakne*), and wonder how to progress to subtler, higher-realm sounds (*sukshma Naad dhun* or *oopari mandalon ki shabd dhun*). They feel stuck, unable to catch the faint, melodious vibrations that mark deeper meditative states.I'll share a practical guide explaining how to move beyond these initial sounds to subtler *Anhad Naad* frequencies, using ear-blocking techniques, focused attention, and mantra chanting (*simran*). This will empower you to deepen your *Anhad Naad sadhana*, align with divine bliss (*anand*), and progress toward *Turiya* (transcendental consciousness) and *Ishwar prapti*.

Meditators practicing *Anhad Naad sadhana* often experience:

- **Limited Sounds**: Hearing only basic sounds (*sannata*, *jheengur*, or bird-like chirps) after prolonged practice, with no progress to subtler sounds (*sukshma dhun*).

- **Frustration**: Inability to "catch" faint, higher-realm sounds (*oopari mandal ki Naad*), which are quieter and harder to perceive.
- **Question**: How to transition from loud, initial sounds to the subtle vibrations that lead to deeper meditative states?

The speaker reassures that initial sounds are a natural starting point, becoming louder with practice, even audible without ear-blocking. However, advancing requires specific techniques to tune into subtler frequencies.

Understanding *Anhad Naad* Progression

- **Initial Sounds**: Sounds like silence, crickets, or chirps are the first layer of *Anhad Naad*, easily heard after regular practice. They're loud and accessible, often without aids like ear plugs or fingers.
- **Subtle Sounds**: Higher-realm sounds (*sukshma Naad*) are faint, melodious, and require refined perception. They're like background whispers behind initial sounds, leading to *Turiya* and divine connection.

- **Challenge**: Subtle sounds are hard to hear without blocking external noise, and shifting focus from loud to faint sounds demands disciplined attention.
- **Goal**: Train the mind to "catch" and follow these subtle vibrations, which draw consciousness into deeper meditative states, ultimately merging with *Parmeshwar*.

The Technique: Progressing to Subtle *Anhad Naad*

Here's a step-by-step method to move beyond initial sounds:

1. Block External Noise Effectively

- **Why**: Subtle *Naad* are faint (*sukshma*), easily drowned by external sounds or ear tension. Blocking ears isolates internal vibrations.
- **How**:
    - Use fingers to gently block ear canals or wear high-quality earbuds. Ensure a snug, comfortable seal without strain.
    - Practice in a quiet environment to minimize background noise.
- **When**: Block ears at the start of meditation, especially when focusing on *Anhad Naad*, to amplify internal sounds.

2. Focus Intensely on Initial Sounds

- **How**:
    - Sit in your meditation posture (*dhyan asan*), close eyes, and block ears.
    - Listen to the loud initial sounds (*sannata*, *jheengur*, chirps) with full attention. Immerse your mind in their rhythm.
    - Avoid distractions or analyzing sounds; simply "be" with them.
- **Why**: Deep focus reveals subtler sounds in the background, like whispers behind a loud hum.

3. Identify and Shift to Subtle Sounds

- **How**:
    - As you focus on initial sounds, notice faint, melodious vibrations in the background. These may sound like:
        - **Bumblebee hum** (*bhanwre ki gunjan*): A soft, buzzing vibration.
        - **Distant train horn**: A low, resonant hum from afar.
        - **Heavy truck tires**: A deep, rolling sound like a heavy vehicle moving on road.

- **Distant music** (*madhur sangeet*): A faint, sweet melody.
  - Gently shift your attention from loud initial sounds to these subtler ones. If they fade, return to initial sounds, then try again when subtle sounds reappear.
- **Practice Tip**: Be patient—subtle sounds may vanish initially as your mind adjusts. Repeatedly toggle between loud and faint sounds to train focus.
- **Why**: Subtle sounds pull consciousness deeper, like tuning a radio to a new frequency (*radio tower frequency*).

4. Continue Mantra Chanting (*Simran*) Initially

- **Why**: Until the mind is fully calm, it struggles to focus on subtle *Naad*. *Simran* quiets mental chatter.
- **How**:
  - Begin meditation with 5–10 minutes of mantra chanting to stabilize the mind.
  - Once calm, shift to listening for *Anhad Naad*, starting with initial sounds and progressing to subtler ones.
  - Don't abandon *simran* until subtle sounds are consistently clear.

- **Advanced Stage**: In higher states (*uchch avastha*), the mind naturally drops *simran*, merging with *Naad*. Until then, use *simran* to anchor focus.

5. Persist with Daily Practice

- **How**:
    - Meditate daily, dedicating 20–30 minutes to *Anhad Naad sadhana*.
    - Consistently block ears, focus on initial sounds, and shift to subtle sounds when detected.
    - Note progress: subtle sounds become clearer (*spasht*) and louder (*teevra*) over weeks, while initial sounds fade.
- **Why**: Regular practice enhances concentration, expanding consciousness (*chitt ka vistar*) to perceive higher-realm *Naad*.

How Subtle Sounds Lead to *Turiya*

- **Mechanism**: Subtle *Naad* vibrations (*sukshma dhun*) draw consciousness into deeper meditative layers, like a radio catching a new station. Each sound leads to the next, pulling you toward *Turiya* (transcendental state).

- **Experience**:
  - Subtle sounds like *bhanwre ki gunjan* may reveal even finer vibrations, such as conch (*shankhnaad*), bell (*ghanta naad*), lute (*veena naad*), or *Om* resonance (*Omkaar gunjan*).
  - These appear briefly, requiring quick focus to "catch" them.
- **Outcome**: Sustained focus on subtle *Naad* induces bliss (*anand*), purifies the mind, controls senses, and fosters a constant connection to *Parmeshwar*.

The Radio Analogy

Imagine *Anhad Naad's* progression to driving between cities:

- **Initial Sounds**: Like music from a nearby radio tower, loud and clear.
- **Subtle Sounds**: Like faint signals from the next city's tower, requiring tuning.
- **Transition**: As you move away from one tower (initial sounds fade), you tune into the next (subtle sounds strengthen). Similarly, deepening meditation shifts focus from loud

Naad to subtler ones, advancing consciousness.

Will Initial Sounds Always Remain Loud?

- **No**: As concentration deepens, initial sounds (*sannata*, *jheengur*) gradually fade, replaced by subtler *Naad* (*sukshma dhun*).
- **Sign of Progress**: When initial sounds diminish, and subtle sounds dominate, you're entering blissful states, feeling anchored to *Parmeshwar*.

Common Questions Answered

1. **Do I need *simran* when initial sounds are loud?**
   - Yes, until subtle *Naad* are clear. *Simran* calms the mind, enabling focus on faint sounds. Drop *simran* only in advanced states.
2. **What if subtle sounds vanish?**
   - Normal initially. Return to initial sounds, then retry when subtle sounds reappear. Patience and practice strengthen perception.
3. **How long until progress?**
   - Varies, but weeks of daily practice (20–30 minutes) with ear-blocking and focus shift subtle sounds from faint to clear, fading initial sounds.

Spiritual Benefits of Subtle *Naad*

- **Blissful Connection**: Subtle *Naad* anchor you in divine bliss (*anand*), feeling *Parmeshwar*'s presence.
- **Mind Purification**: They cleanse mental impurities, control senses, and stabilize consciousness.
- **Path to *Turiya***: Subtle vibrations guide you to transcendental consciousness (*Turiya avastha*), the pinnacle of *Anhad Naad sadhana*.

Practical Tips

- **Environment**: Meditate in a quiet space to minimize external noise.
- **Ear-Blocking**: Experiment with fingers or earbuds for a comfortable seal. Adjust if ears feel strained.
- **Patience**: Subtle sounds may take days or weeks to stabilize. Persist with love (*prem*) and faith (*shraddha*).

Closing Chapter: The Journey Within Continues

There is no true end to a journey that leads inward.

This book was never meant to teach you all there is to know—but to whisper that there *is* something to be remembered. That your longing is real. That your tears are not a weakness but a doorway. That your silence has a sound, and your darkness holds a light.

If you've reached this final page, perhaps something stirred in you—a familiarity, a pull, a wordless ache. That ache is the Maalik calling. It is not a sign of distance, but nearness. Not absence, but love knocking from the inside.

You may still feel unworthy. You may still forget past lives, old promises, the deeper reason you were sent here. But your Maalik has not forgotten. He watches over your breath, your stumbling steps, your half-said prayers. Every moment of remembrance is returned with a thousand blessings. Every cry reaches Him. Every silence is heard.

If this book has done anything, let it be this: that you now sit in stillness not with discipline, but with devotion. That you close your eyes not to escape, but to come Home. That you understand—*even if no memory rises in you, your Guru remembers you perfectly.*

This is not the end.
You are being remembered, called, and loved.
Sit again. Listen again. The silence still sings.

Poem: The One Who Waited

He saw me fall through time and dust,
And still He kept His silent trust.
Though lifetimes passed and paths grew dim,
I had forgotten—but not Him.

He saw me born with veiled eyes,
He watched me search the starless skies.
Each time I ran, He stood so still,
Love holding fast beyond my will.

I don't recall the vows I made,
Or songs in ancient silence played.
But He remembers every tone,
Each word I whispered, each step alone.

Now when I cry, it's not with shame,
But love that calls Him by no name.
And in that cry, the veil must fall—
I know He's heard, I know He'll call.

So I will walk this path unseen,
Through shadowed woods and fields between.
Until that Light calls me inside,
Where no more "you" and "I" divide.

He waited once, He waits still now—
With timeless grace upon His brow.
And when I reach the inner shore,
I'll find I was alone no more.

Glossary of Terms

Adi Shakti
The primordial divine feminine energy, revered as the origin of all creation. Often associated with Kundalini in yogic and mystical traditions.

Ajna Chakra
Also known as the third eye, it is an energy center between the eyebrows linked to intuition and inner vision. Meditation often focuses on this point for deeper awareness.

Anhad Naad
Literally "unstruck sound"; the divine inner sound heard during deep meditation. It is not produced externally and is central to spiritual awakening in this practice.

Anhat
Unstruck or not caused by any two objects colliding. It refers to the spiritual sound that arises from within and connects one to the divine.

Ang Sang
A state of feeling the divine presence with you at all times — "with every limb," or pervasively present.

Atma Vichar
Self-inquiry; the inner questioning of "Who am I?" used to explore one's true nature beyond the body and mind.

Bhakti
Loving devotion to a deity, guru, or the divine. Considered a powerful force for spiritual transformation.

Chitta Shuddhi
Purification of the mind and consciousness, a necessary condition for deep meditation and union with the divine.

Chetana Shakti
Consciousness energy; the inner life force that becomes active and focused during meditation.

Divya Prakash
Divine inner light seen during meditation, symbolizing spiritual illumination.

Guru Shabd / Simran
A mantra given by the guru for repetition during meditation. "Simran" refers to the loving remembrance of this divine name.

Ida and Pingala Nadis

Two primary energy channels in the body, balancing feminine (cooling) and masculine (heating) energies. Their harmony is essential in yogic practices.

Ishwar Prapti

Attainment or realization of the Supreme Being; the goal of many spiritual paths.

Ishta Devta

One's personal deity or divine form to whom devotion is directed, such as Krishna, Shiva, or Guru Nanak.

Jap / Japa

The act of mantra repetition — aloud, with the breath, or silently — to focus the mind and connect with the divine.

Kaam, Krodh, Lobh, Moh, Ahankaar

The five enemies of the mind in Indian spirituality: Lust, Anger, Greed, Attachment, and Ego.

Kul Malik / Maalik

The Supreme Lord or Source; often used with deep love and reverence to refer to the divine.

Maya

The illusion or deceptive appearance of the material world, which distracts from spiritual truth.

Moksha

Liberation from the cycle of birth and death; ultimate spiritual freedom.

Param Pad / Paramatma

The supreme state or Supreme Soul — the highest goal of spiritual realization.

Prem

Pure love, often divine or unconditional. Essential for progress on the spiritual path.

Samadhi

A state of total meditative absorption where the self merges with the divine. Comes in stages — initial focus and complete merging.

Samarpan

Surrender; offering one's ego and will to the divine or guru with humility and trust.

Sampoorna Vishwas

Complete faith; trusting fully in the guru or divine presence.

Sansarik Samasya

Worldly problems; often contrasted with spiritual challenges in the book.

Sant Gyan

Wisdom of saints; deep spiritual insight passed down through realized masters.

Siddhi

Supernatural or mystical

power attained through advanced spiritual practice — often discouraged unless guided by a true guru.

Sushupti

Deep sleep state; sometimes used metaphorically to describe mental stillness in meditation.

Tadap

Intense spiritual longing — a burning desire for union with the divine.

Turiya

The fourth state of consciousness beyond waking, dreaming, and deep sleep — pure awareness.

Virah

Spiritual yearning or separation from the divine, often expressed as longing in devotional poetry or meditation.

✧ *Your Reflections* ✧

Use this space to write what arises within you as you walk the inner path.
What did you feel? What did you remember? What did Maalik whisper in silence?